4.75

Critical Guides to French Texts

79 Butor: La Modification

Critical Guides to French Texts

EDITED BY ROGER LITTLE, WOLFGANG VAN EMDEN,
DAVID WILLIAMS

BUTOR

La Modification

Jean H. Duffy

Lecturer in French
University of Sheffield

Grant & Cutler Ltd
1990

I.S.B.N. 84-599-2932-9

DEPÓSITO LEGAL: V. 247 - 1990

Printed in Spain by
Artes Gráficas Soler, S. A., Valencia

for

GRANT & CUTLER LTD
55-57, GREAT MARLBOROUGH STREET, LONDON W1V 2AY

To my mother and in memory of my father

Contents

Contents

Prefatory Note

P A G E references in the text are to the edition in the Collection Double, Paris: Minuit, 1985. Italicised numbers in parentheses, followed by page references, refer to the numbered items in the select bibliography at the end of this volume.

I should like to thank the following: Professors David Williams and Roger Little, who read the manuscript and offered invaluable advice and constructive criticism; the staff of the Taylor Institution Library, Oxford and the Library of the University of Sheffield.

Sheffield, 1989   JHD

Biographical Note

M I C H E L Butor (born 1926) comes from a practising Catholic family and was himself a pupil of the Collège des Jésuites
at Evreux. A student of both literature and philosophy, he
was awarded his *licence* in philosophy in 1946. He went on to
prepare a diploma on 'Les mathématiques et l'idée de néces-
sité' under Gaston Bachelard and planned to write a doctoral
thesis on 'Les aspects de l'ambiguïté en littérature et l'idée de
signification' – titles which indicated at an early stage some of
Butor's central interests. Since 1950, he has travelled exten-
sively (Germany, Italy, Greece, USA, Brazil, New Mexico)
and taught in schools and universities in Egypt, Manchester,
Greece, Switzerland and the USA) – experiences which have
contributed to his already impressive erudition and which
undoubtedly strengthened his acute interest in questions of
time and space. Butor is an extremely prolific writer, and this
repertoire includes novels, poetry, essays and art criticism. In
recent years he has largely abandoned the novel form in
favour of poetry – a fairly logical development in terms of his
own evolution and his increasing interest over the years in
the possibilities of linguistic patterning.

La Modification, which was published in 1957 and won
the Prix Renaudot in the same year, lies squarely within
Butor's *nouveau roman* period and is a fine example of the
tension between story and experiment which characterised
much of the literature of the fifties.

1

Literary Context: the *Nouveau Roman*

T H E critical label *nouveau roman* is deceptive to the extent
that it suggests a coherent literary movement with a common
policy. Like the Theatre of the Absurd, the *nouveau roman*
is not a literary school and there is no single manifesto to
which all the writers concerned would subscribe. Individually
the writers are all quite different from one another. Their
early careers were quite distinct and by the time critics were
beginning to talk about the *nouveau roman* in the fifties,
many of the writers concerned were into their middle age and
had been writing for some time.

The disparate composition of the *nouveau roman* is,
however, also due to a quite conscious reluctance on the part
of individual authors to form a new orthodoxy: 'Songeons au
nouveau roman: ce n'est pas un groupe, ni une école. On ne
lui connaît pas de chef de collectif, de revue, de manifeste...
Point d'orthodoxie confortable, donc, à laquelle on puisse se
conformer'. [1]

The question of the writers covered by the term *nouveau
roman* constitutes another problem. In the past, critical
studies have included in this category idiosyncratic and probably unclassifiable writers such as Marguerite Duras and
Samuel Beckett. However, in general, critical discussion has
settled down to the point where one can identify a hard core
of writers with related priorities and common critical dislikes
who are themselves willing to be called *nouveaux romanciers.*
Such are Claude Simon, Nathalie Sarraute, Michel Butor,
Alain Robbe-Grillet, Jean Ricardou, Robert Pinget, Claude
Ollier and Claude Mauriac. These writers, while evolving in

[1] J. Ricardou, *Le Nouveau Roman,* Paris: Seuil, 1973, p. 6.

quite distinctive ways, agree on a sufficient number of substantial points to give the critical term *nouveau roman* a
currency value.

All of these writers reject the traditional view of language
as being a relatively unproblematical vehicle for the representation of reality. One objection frequently raised by them
concerns the discrepancy between our instantaneous perception of a multitude of things at any one moment and the fact
that when we describe it we have to resort to a linear
medium, one in which the meaning is created and perceived
in units occupying a certain amount of time. This means that
the information received by the senses has to be given a
certain order of description which is not intrinsic to the
perception and which does not translate the simultaneity
of the impressions. The narrators of *L'Emploi du temps* and
Degrés, both written by Butor, are obsessed with the *décalage*
between experience and recording. Not only is their material
unwieldy, but as they are writing, new events are happening
around them multiplying relentlessly the number of data to
be taken into account.

The *nouveaux romanciers* further recognise that description is potentially infinite in the sense that any scene could
be broken into ever smaller units and more and more detail
supplied. By drawing attention to the fact there could never
be a definitive transcription of reality, the *nouveau roman*
also exposes the selectivity and non-objectivity of Realist
description. The Balzacian description may seem long, but in
Simon or Butor's work the elaboration of ever-ramifying
digressions and analysis suggests the multitude of factors to be
considered in the description of an apparently simple situation.

The *nouveaux romanciers* also reject any concept of
literature which reduces it to the status of a medium for the
propagation of a message about the world. In his essay 'Sur
quelques notions périmées', Robbe-Grillet argues that whereas revolutionary or committed literature would require that
every other consideration be subordinated to the cause, the
artist, at the moment of writing, cannot concern himself with

anything but his art.[2] Claude Simon has likewise condemned any attempt to turn literature into a medium for conveying a certain philosophy of life. Any criterion can serve as a basis for judgement and every ideology is simply the arbitrary adoption of one point of view from among many: 'On peut baser une philosophie et une conception de la vie sur à peu près n'importe quoi, sur n'importe quelle obsession ...et en faire découler tout un système logique ou onirique'.[3]

The writers of the *nouveau roman* do, however, propose a less ambitious social role for the writer. They argue that formal experimentation can make the reader see the world anew. One of Butor's principal interests is the way in which man perceives and records time. He is fascinated by the multitude of real and potential relationships to be established among different points in time. In *Degrés,* the narrator starts off with the apparently straightforward intention of describing an hour in the life of his class. However, it soon emerges that to do this with accuracy he is going to require more and more information about the pupils and their lives and that the description of the subject being taught requires that he allude to a humanly unmanageable amount of material and systems of reference. Ann Jefferson sums up the problem very well: 'The hour itself disappears in the network of systems which structure the way in which we make sense of it until finally it exists simply as a pivot'.[4] What had started off as an apparently simple task is revealed to be a problem of quite mind-boggling complexity. *Degrés* exemplifies a very important statement made by Butor in 'Le Roman comme recherche' where he argues that novelistic form should not only be changing to match the fast-changing world but also that new forms will make us aware of previously unseen relationships between the novel and reality (*11,* p. 10).

[2] *Pour un nouveau roman,* Paris: Minuit, 1963, pp. 33-39.
[3] *La Corde raide,* Paris: Sagittaire, 1947, p. 95.
[4] *The Nouveau Roman and the Poetics of Fiction,* Cambridge: CUP, 1980, p. 155.

Although the *nouveau roman* can be readily charged with political irresponsibility because of its reluctance to align itself with any specific ideological position, it does share with contemporary political and sociological thinkers an interest in the way in which our view of the world is conditioned by cultural codes:

> A chaque instant, des franges de culture (psychologie, morale, métaphysique, etc.) viennent s'ajouter aux choses, leur donnant un aspect moins étranger, plus compréhensible. Nous sommes habitués à ce que cette littérature... fonctionne comme une grille, munie de verres diversement colorés, qui décompose notre champ de perception en petits carreaux assimilables.[5]

Our conception of the novel too is, according to the *nouveau roman,* conditioned by our reading of the literature of other generations. This conditioning contributes to stagnation in the creative process. Hence, they claim, contemporary popular fiction and the literature of social realism are based on outdated assumptions deriving from nineteenth-century Realism. Our concept of the realistic is based not on reality but on past representations of reality.

Their interest in codes and their desire to expose the purely cultural status of Realism manifests itself in a fairly sustained programme of debunking. All of the *nouveaux romanciers* spend a good deal of energy demonstrating the technical tricks on which 'realism' rests. The *nouveau roman* is above all a self-reflexive form. The main 'theme' is the activity of writing and the reader is never allowed to become completely caught up in the plot or identify with the characters. He is at all times aware of the way in which the narrative is composed. The fiction is constantly drawing attention to its status as fiction; a meditation upon literature, genre, language, structure and time, it spurns easy consumption.

---

[5] *Pour un nouveau roman,* p. 18.

2

Ideas and Aims

O f the writing normally classified as the *nouveau roman,* Michel Butor's work is possibly the most cerebral. Certainly, his novels and essays do not propose a coherent philosophy of life nor a moral commentary on the world. Nevertheless, their conception and composition owe a great deal to Butor's own philosophical training, and much of his fiction is under-pinned by questions relating to time and space, perception and representation. Butor himself has made it quite clear that he saw in the novel a way of reconciling poetry and philo-sophy, a way of bridging the gulf between the poetry he wrote as a student – 'une poésie de désarroi, très irrationaliste' (*11,* p. 15) – and his ambition to shed some light on the philo-sophical questions which he was studying. In the novel, Butor sought to marry poetic stylisation with one of the most influential philosophical schools of the period – phenom-enology. Style, methodical description and, above all, formal experimentation are, according to Butor, a means of renewing our perception of the world, of making us aware of things and responses which we take for granted.

The notion of phenomenological reduction consists in the suspension of our utilitarian view of the world, the neutralisation of the codes which automatise our attitude to the world.

La meilleure formule de la réduction est sans doute celle qu'en donnait Eugen Fink, l'assistant de Husserl, quand il parlait d'un 'étonnement' devant le monde. La réflexion ne se retire pas du monde... elle distend les fils intentionnels qui nous relient au monde pour les faire paraître, elle seule est

conscience du monde parce qu'elle le révèle comme étrange et
paradoxale.[6]

Significantly both Merleau-Ponty and Butor have designated
the novel as a propitious experimental field in which to effect
the suspension of those blunting, self-evident truths which
preclude pristine perception: 'La vraie philosophie est de
rapprendre à voir le monde, et en ce sens une histoire
racontée peut signifier le monde avec autant de "profondeur"
qu'un traité de philosophie';[7] '[le roman] est le domaine
phénoménologique par excellence, le lieu par excellence où
étudier de quelle façon la réalité nous apparaît ou peut nous
apparaître; c'est pourquoi le roman est le laboratoire du récit'
(*11*, p. 9). The exploration of form is, like phenomenological
reduction, a way of disrupting perceptual habits and reflexes
and of throwing into question the assumptions which inherit-
ed knowledge, hearsay and the representations of previous
generations have instilled in us.

Most *nouveaux romanciers* are agreed upon the idea that
past representations of reality condition our view of the world
to the extent that we confuse the world with what we have
been told about it: 'C'est en grande partie à travers les livres,
les romans notamment, que nous connaissons l'univers...
Dans notre représentation, ce que nous voyons de nos yeux
tient fort peu de place par rapport à ce dont on parle' (*10*,
p. 8). The only valid form of literature, according to the *nouveau roman,* is the one which, while accepting the fact that it
too will date, nevertheless tries to make us aware of the
contingency, distortions and omissions of previous representations and obliges us to look again at the world around us:
'L'exploration de formes romanesques différentes révèle ce
qu'il y a de contingent dans celle à laquelle nous sommes
habitúes, la démasque, nous en délivre, nous permet de
retrouver au-delà de ce récit fixe tout ce qu'il camoufle ou
qu'il tait, tout ce récit fondamental dans lequel baigne notre

[6] M. Merleau-Ponty, *Phénoménologie de la perception,* Paris: Gallimard,
1945, p. viii.
[7] Merleau-Ponty, p. xvi.

vie entière' (*11*, pp. 9-10). Here, once again, Butor comes very close to the thinking of Merleau-Ponty and his concept of the 'parole authentique' which will render possible the temporary transcendence of our coded perspective: 'La parole fait lever un sens nouveau, si elle est parole authentique... D'ailleurs, il faut bien que les significations maintenant acquises aient été des significations nouvelles'.[8] Considered in this perspective, it seems likely that the 'modification' heralded in the title of Butor's third novel refers not only to Léon Delmont's change of mind but also to a qualitative change in the way in which both Léon and the reader view the world and their situation in it.

The choice of a train-journey as the fictional structure is not without significance in this respect. *La Modification* must be viewed as part of a long tradition of imaginary journeys. What is especially interesting about this particular novel is its play on two different types of imaginary journey. Léon's plans at the outset of *La Modification* suggest that we are dealing with the well-tried formula of the attempt to recapture some kind of lost paradise, in this case Classical Rome: 'le voyage au site oraculaire; on y apporte sa question, on en attend une réponse, guérison du corps et de l'âme. Le lieu saint se détache au milieu de régions profanes; il est la lucarne sur le paradis' (*12*, p. 19). In the course of the novel, it becomes clear, however, that *La Modification* is to be classified in another quite different category of imaginary journey – the journey as pretext for a fresh and critical assessment of a particular set of assumptions and values whether they be social and historical (as in Montesquieu's *Lettres Persanes*) or personal (as in the case of Gide's *L'Immoraliste*). In *La Modification* the journey gives Léon the opportunity for some 'time out' in which he can reflect on both his personal concerns and their place within the broad historical context. This trip, instead of bringing an easy 'réponse', poses questions.

The physical conditions of the journey itself act as catalysts for reflection. First of all, the timing of the journey and

[8] Merleau-Ponty, p. 226.

the choice of travelling class represent a deviation from
Léon's routine. The day-to-day professional activities which
dominate his life are temporarily suspended and he is able to
distance himself somewhat from his situation. The temporary
liberation from the tasks which normally occupy his thoughts
and structure his time means that he is free to observe with
increased awareness the details of his immediate *Lebenswelt*[9]
and his own sensory impressions. This hypersensitivity to
details of which, in the normal run of things, León would be
only marginally aware is in part due to his state of enforced
inactivity. His body is, as it were, in a state of suspended
animation – he is not acting upon the world, but his body
continues to perceive the way in which the world is acting
upon it. Furthermore, his mind is now free to process and
formulate peripheral perceptions from the preceding days
when he was otherwise occupied: 'Quand vous êtes entré dans
la salle à manger mercredi pour déjeuner (à travers la fenêtre
brillaient les admirables rinceaux de la frise du Panthéon
éclairés d'un rayon de soleil blanc de novembre qui s'est vite
terni)' (p. 35).

La Modification is peppered with references to minute
sensory details and meticulous descriptions of the movements
involved in very basic gestures not normally described in
novels. Butor's interest in the way in which we perceive our
immediate surroundings results frequently in an impression-
istic technique whereby the narrator avoids naming even the
most minor and banal incidents in an attempt to convey the
way in which the world appears to our senses, the pre-
recognition perception. The reader is, for example, not told
that the train has moved off; the event is simply recorded in
terms of what impinges on Léon's vision: 'Au-delà de la
fenêtre la gare d'Aix-les-Bains se remet en branle, s'en va'
(p. 133), 'L'espace extérieur s'agrandit brusquement, c'est
une locomotive minuscule qui s'approche et qui disparaît
(pp. 12-13). The process of perception may be impeded by the

[9] The term 'Lebenswelt' ('life-world') is used by Edmund Husserl and
Maurice Merleau-Ponty to refer to the world of lived experience as perceived
by a subjectivity located in time and space.

number of screens or obstacles between the perceiver and the perceived, resulting in a delay in the recognition of a common object: 'De l'autre côté du corridor, au travers de la vitre couverte de toute une toile tissée par les gouttes de pluie, vous devinez à cette luisance d'aluminium que ce qui s'approche, vous croise et disparaît, c'était un camion' (p. 97). The narrator often treats causes and effects simply as discrete impressions: 'La poignée que vous teniez dans votre main s'anime; la porte s'ouvre; un homme passe la tête, puis referme' (p. 267). Here only the last word of the sentence establishes an explicit link between the man and the opening and shutting of the carriage door. Until then the inanimate object seemed to have a life of its own. The fact that Léon can see only fragments of the people who pass along the corridor results in a similar animation of banal articles of clothing: 'une manche d'imperméable balaie le carreau auquel votre tempe s'appuie toujours, puis un volumineux sac à main de nylon noir avec un bouton de galalithe y frappe quelques coups' (p. 20).

Occasionally, the apparent 'independence' of the objects is such that they constitute considerable obstacles to the human beings who conceived of them for their own convenience. Thus the problems encountered by various passengers trying to open the heavy carriage door is a recurring motif. What this motif points to, I think, is the fact that the object (even the man-made object) retains a certain opacity and resistance to human physical or intellectual control which tend to be forgotten in our day-to-day anthropocentric and functional perspective on these objects:

> On ne peut... concevoir de chose perçue sans quelqu'un qui la perçoive. Mais encore est-il que la chose se présente à celui-là même qui la perçoit comme chose en soi et qu'elle pose le problème d'un véritable en-soi-pour-nous. Nous ne nous en avisons pas d'ordinaire parce que notre perception, dans le contexte de nos occupations, se pose sur les choses juste assez pour redécouvrir ce qui s'y cache d'inhumain.[10]

[10] Merleau-Ponty, p. 372.

According to Heidegger the malfunctioning or breakdown of a tool (i.e. an object considered essentially as being subordinated to the purposes of man) exposes the fallacy of the anthropocentric assumption of superiority over one's environment. Here the combination of the stiff door and the reduction in the control the passengers have over their movements in the unstable environment of the moving train is used to highlight the complexity of gestures and actions to which we would normally pay little attention. In the journey, the individual is not only distanced from his habitual surroundings but he is rendered physically more vulnerable. In everyday circumstances Léon would seem to be a man who is in control of his life and to have a certain amount of power – the physical conditions of his trip play an important part in the subversion of his self-assurance.

The choice of the journey is also related to Butor's self-confessed didacticism. Butor's didacticism does not consist in communicating a certain ideological position on the world, but rather in questioning existing assumptions and standpoints with a view to indirectly changing the world: 'Toutes les grandes œuvres... transforment la façon dont nous voyons et racontons le monde, et par conséquent le monde' (*11*, p. 112). The fictional journey stands as a kind of metaphor for the distanciation from one's own situation involved in all reading. As the reader is drawn out of his own world and projected imaginatively into another time and space he is afforded a new perspective on the world:

> La station que représente le lieu décrit dans ce voyage d'aller et retour inhérent à toute lecture peut avoir avec l'endroit où je me trouve des relations spatiales fort diverses; la distance romanesque n'est pas seulement une évasion, elle peut introduire dans l'espace vécu des modifications tout à fait originales. (*11*, p. 51)

> Toute fiction s'inscrit... en notre espace comme voyage, et l'on peut dire à cet égard que c'est là le thème fondamental de toute littérature romanesque; tout roman qui nous raconte un voyage est donc plus clair, plus explicite que celui qui n'est pas capable d'exprimer métaphoriquement cette distance

entre le lieu de la lecture et celui où nous emmène le récit. (*11*, p. 50)

The reader, like Léon, is freed temporarily from humdrum daily preoccupations and invited to consider other aspects, times and places. Butor, himself an avid reader of Jules Verne, describes this process in 'Le Voyage et l'écriture': 'Ce lieu qui se déplace fournit le retrait demandé par rapport aux enchaînements quotidiens' (*12*, p. 12).

It is this concern to draw the reader into another's situation which determines in part the use of the second person plural form. Experimentation with narrative point of view is a well-known feature of the *nouveau roman*. In *La Route des Flandres* Claude Simon is constantly operating shifts from first to third person narration in an attempt to convey the discontinuity of the self in time and the instability of memory. Robbe-Grillet's *La Jalousie* is a technical tour de force which creates the illusion of an intensely subjective narratorial presence without, however, using the pronoun 'je'. In *La Modification,* the highly unusual choice of the second person form of narration gives prominence to the author's appeal for attention: 'Or, si le romancier publie son livre... c'est qu'il a absolument besoin du lecteur pour le mener à bien, comme complice de sa constitution... comme personne, intelligence et regard' (*11*, p. 17). In *La Modification,* as in the *nouveau roman* in general, the reader is a crucial element in the production of meaning. The reader is not simply the passive recipient of a story or a predigested view of the world. He has to work to make sense of what he is reading. The multiple questions posed by the Grand Veneur to Léon are also addressed to the reader, make him examine his preconceptions about his identity and desires. The readers of *La Modification* may not move from their chairs but they are offered a new perspective which effects an imaginary displacement: 'Le seul véritable voyage... ce ne serait pas d'aller vers de nouveaux paysages, mais d'avoir d'autres yeux, de voir l'univers avec les yeux d'un autre' (*5*, p. 169).

Of course, *La Modification* can also be seen as a variation on the theme of the voyage of self-discovery. On one level it is obviously the story of an individual caught up in the eternal triangle of adultery and, as we shall see later in the analysis of Léon's character, the moral dimension of this question does not fail to interest Butor. Furthermore, Léon's physical trip is matched by a mental and emotional journey: 'le mouvement qui s'est produit dans votre esprit accompagnant le déplacement de votre corps d'une gare à l'autre à travers tous les paysages intermédiaires' (pp. 285-86). In the course of his deliberations he comes to realise the vanity of his initial plans to leave Henriette and bring Cécile to Paris. He has made this journey between Rome and Paris so often that every point along the way is saturated with personal associations which he cannot keep at bay. Gradually, as pleasant and unpleasant memories relating to both relationships spring to mind, his idealistic conception of the planned new life with Cécile is relativised and he realises that he would simply be repeating the history of his relationship with Henriette. The journey is an obvious choice of context for such deliberations. Nothing concrete can be done, but life-changing decisions can be made and unmade.

However, more important, I would suggest, than the resolution of a personal dilemma (i.e. the stuff of the traditional psychological novel) is the broadening of Léon's perception of his own case, the realisation of the representative dimension of his relationship with these two women and the recognition of his own historical situation. One of the most important things which León comes to realise in the course of his trip is that his plans were based on an illusion – the assumption that the solution to his problems lay with one woman, Cécile, and that most of his problems were due to the stagnation of his relationship with his wife. By the end of the journey he recognises that his attraction to Cécile is inextricably bound up with the Roman context in which their love took root. Ultimately, Cécile is less important as an individual than as what she represents for him – the pagan side of Rome, its promotion of the beautiful and enjoyable aspects of life. Similarly, Henriette with whom he has made two trips to Rome represents the Catholic side of the City of Cities. Both he and Cécile see Catholicism as repression, as the obstacle to the fulfilment of their plans. Thus, he feels obliged to avoid scandalising the Catholic firm for which he works while Cécile sees the Vatican as representative of all that stands in the way of their happiness. Léon joins Cécile in her condemnation of Catholicism and would seem, in the first part of the novel, to be turning his back on it. However, it becomes clear that he is unaware of the hold that it has over him. He has obviously not reckoned with what Butor sees as the deep-seated Catholicism of French culture: 'Tout Français est nourri de catholicisme dès son berceau ... le sol ... sur lequel tout repose, c'est quand même le catholicisme' (*44*, p. 17) – a point already made in the early *Passage de Milan* where the tenement which forms the pivot of the novel is built above an old church. Léon assumes that his particular attraction to Rome is personal and specific to himself. In fact, of course, he is just one of many – among them Dante, Panini, Montaigne, Freud – who throughout history have been susceptible to the eternal city's magnetic force of suggestion. What Léon had failed to realise in the midst of his personal and business worries and in spite of his extensive sight-seeing is the extent to which our mental processes are conditioned by the cultural framework into which we are born.

The effect Catholicism has had on Léon is apparent to the reader before it is to Léon. His refusal to kiss Cécile outside his office may at first seem to be prompted by a desire to avoid scandal. However, a neatly parallel situation on pages 172-73 where he refuses to kiss in the church is surely evidence of underlying religious scruples about his adulterous relationship. Furthermore, there is a certain perverse authorial irony in the fact that Léon's Christian name and surname remind us of a whole host of popes and of the hill on which the Vatican is built, while the two women in his life bear the names of two Christian heroines: 'Cécile was a Christian martyr in Imperial Rome and ... Henriette was a French princess who was instrumental in the re-establishment of Roman Catholicism in England in the 17th century!' (*49*, p. 8).

But undoubtedly the clearest indication of a certain Catholic loyalty is to be found in his repeated and frequently recalled arguments with Cécile over the question of visiting the Vatican. In his initial reference to the fact that they have visited neither the Vatican nor St Peter's together, Léon suggests that Cécile's more extreme anti-clericalism is the very reason why he loves her so much (p. 58). Even after the evocation of the open confrontation with Cécile on page 168 where she tells him he is riddled with Catholicism, Léon still refuses to acknowledge its hold: 'il était bien impossible, bien inutile de lui expliquer qu'elle n'y était pas du tout, d'essayer de lui donner des idées raisonnables'. However, the repeated references to this omission and to the various religious works of art of the Vatican signal its importance in Léon's subconscious. The work of art to which Léon attaches most importance is significantly Michelangelo's *Last Judgement,* a harrowing work which offers the impenitent sinner no comfort. It is to it and all that it represents that the narrator refers when he evokes the feeling of a gap during Cécile's and Léon's visit to Saint-Pietro-in-Vincoli. Here Michelangelo's *Moses* is but a pale reflection of something which deep down preoccupies Léon. The *Last Judgement* is a symbol of what is and would be missing in a life with Cécile (p. 173). It is significantly only a few pages later that Cécile refers to another unspoken issue lurking under the surface and dividing them – he has never spoken to her of his life in Paris. The relationship is in a sense founded on omissions. With Cécile, Henriette and the Vatican are both taboo subjects, a parallel which highlights the connection between the Vatican and his life with Henriette. His decision to stay with Henriette and his recognition of the importance of Christian Rome are inextricable.

It would be a mistake, however, to label *La Modification* as a Christian novel or to see Léon's modification as a reconversion. Léon's case is that of a modern man who 'ne saura plus exactement quels sont les moments importants, hésitera entre deux ou trois ensembles de fêtes, de temples, de prêtres; il ne saura plus comment il convient de consacrer les nœuds de sa propre vie, à quel dieu s'adresser, se vouer' (*11,* p. 35). The question to which Léon addresses himself on page 191 – 'à quel saint, quelle sainte me [vouer]' is an expression of this dilemma. Léon's mistake was not to stray from the path of Christian righteousness but to repress the effect that his Catholic education had on his view of things. He was mistaken when he assumed that Classical Rome with its pagan values was his 'lieu de l'authenticité' (p. 146). That was to promote one side of his temperament, the sensual, at the expense of his conscience.

The most important discovery which Léon makes in this novel is that in the twentieth century there is no single moral or cultural centre to our world. The twentieth-century view of things is relativistic and Léon's realisation of this is part of a general historical *prise de conscience*:

> Une des grandes vagues de l'histoire s'achève ainsi dans vos consciences, celle où le monde avait un centre, qui n'était pas seulement la terre au milieu des sphères de Ptolomée, mais Rome au centre de la terre, un centre qui s'est déplacé, qui a cherché à se fixer après l'écroulement de Rome à Byzance, puis beaucoup plus tard dans le Paris impérial ... le souvenir de l'empire est maintenant une figure insuffisante pour désigner l'avenir de ce monde, devenu pour chacun de nous beaucoup plus vaste et tout autrement distribué. (p. 279)

There are no longer any absolute guidelines about how one should conduct one's life, no depository of values that is universally recognised.

This lack of a centre and the corresponding conflict of cultures manifest themselves even in the banal details of Léon's life. There is a certain irony in the fact that when he is in Paris he drinks at a 'bar romain' (p. 75) and when he is in Rome he goes to see a French film (p. 11-17). And of course since this, it would seem, is a generalised phenomenon, the habits of those around him show similar tell-tale signs. Thus in her room in Rome Cécile has pinned photographs of the Obelisk and the Arc de Triomphe while Scabelli, Léon's employer, frequents the Café de Paris in Rome. All of these examples simply illustrate what Butor sees as a general human tendency: 'Lorsque le voyageur est loin de chez lui ... c'est de sa patrie qu'il rêve alors, elle lui manque et lui apparaît sous des couleurs toutes renouvelées' (*11,*

p. 50). The belief in a spiritual and cultural home would seem to be ever-elusive wish-fulfilment corresponding to a fundamental nostalgia for a solution. It is a need which is not exhaustible by rationality – Léon recognises in advance that in the book he intends to write he will not be able to explain the role of Rome in his/our consciousness: 'sans qu'il puisse être question d'apporter une réponse à cette énigme que désigne dans notre conscience ou notre inconscience le nom de Rome...' (p. 276).

Léon's recognition of his historical situation and the use in the foregoing quotation of the first person plural 'nous' testifies to another important coincidence between the thought of a phenomenologist such as Merleau-Ponty and Butor. Both subscribe, it would seem, to the notion of an intersubjective culture to which we all belong, a historical situation which conditions our freedom of choice.

> Il nous faut donc redécouvrir, après le monde naturel, le monde social, non comme objet ou somme d'objets, mais comme champ permanent ou dimension d'existence ... La conscience objective et scientifique du passé et des civilisations serait impossible si je n'avais avec eux, par l'intermédiaire de ma société, de mon monde culturel et de leurs horizons, une communication au moins virtuelle ... si je ne trouvais dans ma vie les structures fondamentales de l'histoire.[11]

Viewed in this light, Léon's decision to stay with Henriette is then part of a more general understanding of the role of transpersonal cultural and historical factors in our perception and behaviour. Ultimately, neither Butor nor Delmont feels qualified to offer either a causal explanation or a judgement on the importance of Catholicism or pagan hedonism in Léon's psyche. Neither Catholicism nor hedonism offers any solution. Catholicism is repeatedly seen as repressive, while as we shall see in our analysis of Léon's character, his plans to live with Cécile are based on sensuality and selfishness.

[11] Merleau-Ponty, p. 415.

Ultimately, Butor is more interested in the codes and structures by which we organise our lives. His didacticism is inextricable from his phenomenological interests and this accounts for the descriptive rather than prescriptive nature of his fiction. He attempts to re-create the conditions governing our perception. Like many of his contemporaries, in particular *nouveaux romanciers* and structuralists, he is content to demonstrate the way in which codes and ideologies function, in the hope no doubt that we distance ourselves sufficiently from our beliefs to avoid self-deception or the confusion of code with reality.

3
The Code

O N E of the ways in which Butor and other *nouveaux romanciers* ensure that we are aware of the way in which cultural codes impinge on and direct our vision of reality is through a proliferation of references to a quite remarkable number of cultural objects and forms of representation. According to Butor, we are surrounded by fiction; our perception is structured by the multitude of narratives told to us and by us every day (*10*, p. 7). What we know about the world depends to a very considerable extent on what we have been told about it: 'C'est en grande partie à travers les livres, les romans notamment, que nous connaissons l'univers' (*10*, p. 8).

In *La Modification* this point is made by the extremely varied reading material of Léon and his fellow-passengers which includes a breviary, railway timetable, guide to Rome, map, woman's magazine, news magazine, library book. The myriad representational forms which surround us are crucial factors in our competent articulation of the mass of data which presents itself to our senses and intelligence. In *La Modification* the importance of the cultural code in the processing of impressions is signalled at numerous points in the text by comparisons drawn from a number of different disciplines.

Elsewhere, the playful attribution of names by Léon to his travelling companions is based largely on his own cultural points of reference:

> ... quant au jeune couple, non, pas d'allusions littéraires, simplement Pierre et, voyons, Cécile est exclu, mais Agnès conviendrait très bien, Sant'Agnese in Agone, l'église de

Borromini sur la Piazza Navona ... Vous vous souvenez de ce
tympan roman de la cathédrale avec le martyr sur le gril, et à
Turin aussi il y a cette coupole de Guarini sur arcs entre-
croisés qui est dédiée à Saint Laurent, donc Lorenzo convien-
drait bien dans les deux cas. (p. 125)

Léon is one of several representative author-figures in Butor.
Butor would seem to be making the point that the story-
teller, whether he be Léon Delmont or Michel Butor, relies
heavily on his own cultural baggage for the data of his fiction.
Butor, like Merleau-Ponty, recognises that the cultured man
cannot exist in a vacuum; he constantly perceives reality
against the backcloth of his previously acquired culture. The
'having seen' of the work of a particular artist is irrevocable
and, whatever his explicit attitude to his heritage, it is one of
implicit acknowledgment:

Il n'y a pas d'art vraiment moderne sans citation parce qu'il y
a l''art moderne' lorsque l'on sait qu'il y a déjà eu beaucoup
de livres, beaucoup de peinture, beaucoup de musique, voire
même que nous sommes encombrés de littérature, de peinture, de musique. (*36*, p. 6)

La peinture de Van Gogh est installée en moi pour toujours,
un pas est fait sur lequel je ne peux pas revenir, et, même si je
ne garde aucun souvenir précis de tableaux que j'ai vus, toute
mon expérience esthétique désormais sera celle de quelqu'un
qui a connu la peinture de Van Gogh. [12]

With his interest in time and space, Butor is, of course,
particularly keen to show the way in which our perception of a
place is conditioned by its cultural associations and he argues
that the attempt to describe the impact a place has on any one
consciousness must take into account its works of art and
culture: 'Dans cette puissance d'un lieu par rapport à un autre,
les œuvres d'art ont toujours joué un rôle particulièrement important, que ce soit peinture ou roman, et par conséquent le
romancier, s'il veut véritablement éclairer la structure de notre
espace, est obligé de les faire intervenir' (*11*, p. 58).

---

[12] Merleau-Ponty, p. 450.

The impossibility of separating the cultures of France and Italy is discreetly indicated by a number of references to artists who were in some way connected with both countries – Poussin and Claude Lorrain, 'les deux Français de Rome' (p. 70) and Panini (p. 64), known for his views of Rome and his connection with the French Academy. Léon attaches particular importance to this last artist, seeing his imaginary reconstructions of ancient Rome as representative of the tension between the old Empire and the Christian church (p. 65). While Rome is primarily associated in Léon's consciousness with Cécile and a kind of pagan freedom and pleasure, he cannot take a step without mentioning a building, monument or work of art which has some sort of association with the Catholic Church. In particular, a remarkable number of the buildings Léon regularly passes are named after powerful Italian families, which included in their number one or more popes. The Borghesi, Barberini, Colonna and Borgia were all papal families. It is highly ironic that Cécile, the anti-papist, works in the Palais Farnese named after another important papal family, while the name of the hotel where Léon and Henriette spent their honeymoon, the Hôtel Quirinal, is reminiscent of the Quirinal Palace, the summer residence of the Popes until 1870.

While these references are important and create around Léon a space which is resonant with associations, they are nevertheless incidental when compared with the four principal cultural points of reference in the book – the legend of the 'Grand Veneur', the letters of Julian the Apostate, the *Aeneid* and the work of Michelangelo.

Le Grand Veneur

The legend of the Grand Veneur is a recurrent motif in *La Modification*. In his *Folklore de France,* Paul Sébillot gives an account of this centuries-old myth associated with the Forest of Fontainebleau among other places:

Certaines forêts sont hantées par des personnages bruyants qui appartiennent à l'autre monde... Le Grand Veneur... est le plus célèbre.... On cherche encore, [dit Sully, cité par Dom Calmet] de quelle nature pouvoit être ce prestige, vu si souvent par tant d'yeux dans la forêt de Fontainebleau; c'étoit un Phantôme environné d'une meute de chiens dont on entendoit les cris, et qu'on voyoit de loin, mais qui disparois-soit lorsqu'on s'approchoit.... M. de Perefixe fait mention de ce Phantôme et il lui fait dire d'une voix rauque, l'une de ces trois paroles: 'M'attendez-vous ou m'entendez-vous ou amandez-vous'. Et l'on croit, dit-il, que c'étoient des jeux de sorciers ou du Malin Esprit.... [Il] serait apparu peu de temps avant la mort si brusque et si singulière du duc et de la duchesse de Bourgogne; d'après des traditions locales, il aurait prédit à Louis XVI sa fin tragique, et plus tard au duc de Berry.[13]

In *La Modification* there is obviously no question of actual death, though one could perhaps see the reference as a herald of a major upheaval in Léon's life. Butor's use of the legend is selective, concentrating as he does on the Phantom's obsessive questioning. In the course of Léon's reflections, this question undergoes an evolution. Initially, Butor remains faithful to the legend as it is recorded by Sébillot. The phantom's question would seem to be 'N'entendez-vous?' (p. 114) or 'Qu'attendez-vous?' (p. 135), the latter question apparently inciting Léon in his plans to bring Cécile to Paris. However, by page 151 (i.e. very close to the centre of the book) it has turned into 'Où êtes-vous?', raising the crucial question about Léon's allegiance to Classical or Christian Rome. By page 183 the question has become 'Etes-vous fou?', the question with which the phantom addressed him on his return to Paris with Henriette after their disastrous second honeymoon in Rome. Culpability for this disaster lay largely with Léon and the ghost's aggressive interrogation is perhaps drawing attention to the folly of assuming that a return to the honeymoon city without any real effort on Léon's part

---

[13] *Folklore de France,* vol. I, Paris: Maisonneuve et Larose, 1968, pp. 274-75.

would be an easy solution to the marital disharmony. By page 220 the Grand Veneur's initial question has been taken up by Charon in Léon's dream. Here, however, the question 'Qu'attendez-vous?' has taken on a different force given Léon's abandonment of his initial project and is combined with the question 'Qui êtes-vous?' Here it seems to urge him on his quest to establish some kind of authenticity. In short, the transformations undergone by this motif reflect the transformation which is taking place in his awareness.

The legend of the Grand Veneur is also included as a representative of native French culture, a Gallic counterbalance to both Classical and Christian Rome. The importance which Léon attaches to Rome should not blind us to the fact that he is also steeped in the folklore of his own country. The legend of the Grand Veneur is a good example of those *récits* which surround us from birth and which have been handed down from generation to generation. Furthermore, the myth Butor has chosen here is not simply a local story but a variation on an archetype – that of the Mesnie Hellequin or Wild Hunt, 'those spectral hunters riding on the wings of the storm and during the wild nights of autumn and winter. To see them, or have them enter your house means death'.[14] In *La Modification,* the legend stands as an example of native Gallic superstition and belief in the supernatural. The tension between Classical liberty and Christian guilt may dominate the text but the recurrent appearance of the Grand Veneur provides another important relativising factor and reveals another set of very different beliefs underpinning Léon's outlook, whether or not he consciously subscribes to them.

THE LETTERS OF JULIAN THE APOSTATE

The principal Classical points of reference in *La Modification* are the letters of Julian the Apostate and Virgil's *Aeneid,* both of which Léon has read on previous journeys to

[14] M. Blaess, 'The *chasseur maudit* in Alsace', *Lore and Language,* 3, 1980, 83.

Rome. Of the two, Julian is the less prominent, figuring only as a reference in a handful of passages (pp. 99, 205, 218-19, 256, 277). Nevertheless, the emperor is thematically important for a number of reasons. Firstly, the case of Julian epitomises the problems faced by historians in their search for the truth amidst a proliferation of different versions: 'The various accounts can be seen to turn back on themselves, to have interrelationships and distinctive differences at the same time. No one account can be entirely rejected or entirely trusted'.[15] Similarly, at the end of *La Modification,* Léon is faced with the near-impossible task of establishing the truth about the great historical fissure of which he is a part. Secondly, Julian's career was inextricably bound up with both Rome and Gaul: Julian served in Gaul between 355 and 360, and it was in Paris in 360 A.D. that he was elevated to the position of co-emperor. Thirdly, there is Julian's conversion from Christianity to paganism, a conversion which mirrors Léon's rejection of Catholicism for the pagan attraction of Rome and Cécile. The letters which Léon reads on his adulterous trips to Rome are marked by a hostility towards Christianity which mirrors Léon's own condemnation of Catholicism. Furthermore, it has been said of Julian that in his enthusiasm for Hellenism he confused culture with religion – a criticism which could also be levelled against Léon. One of the important things he has to learn is that for twentieth-century man neither paganism nor Catholicism holds the 'truth' but that both are ineradicable elements in his consciousness.

The dreams and visions which appear at decisive moments in the lives of both is another similarity, as is the fact that they both ultimately commit themselves to a life of austere hard work and the pursuit of self-knowledge. Indeed, Julian's advice to the Cynic could almost stand as a statement of some of the aspects of his life which Léon has to re-examine in the course of the novel: 'He who is entering on the career of a Cynic ought first to censure severely and

[15] G. W. Bowersock, *Julian the Apostate,* London: Duckworth, 1978, p. 3.

cross-examine himself, and without any self-flattery ask himself the following question in precise terms; whether he
enjoys expensive food; whether he cannot do without a soft
bed; whether he is the slave of rewards and the opinions of
men'. [16] At the outset of the novel, Léon presents himself as a
successful executive who enjoys a relatively high level of
material comfort. Here Léon's self-image depends on external
contingent things such as wealth, professional standing and
other people's conception of him. However, by half-way
through the novel, he is beginning to see the aridity of his
lifestyle. This disillusionment is a crucial stage in his reassessment of his situation, a reassessment which will result in the
pursuit of a more authentic and personally valid way of life.

The *Aeneid*

The most important Classical point of reference in *La
Modification* is undoubtedly the *Aeneid*. Explicit reference is
made to it several times, while the description on page 204 of
one of Léon's travelling companions is also a clear allusion:
'ce vieillard en face de vous, dont les yeux ne sont pas tout à
fait fermés et qui a l'air de se réciter à lui-même quelque long
poème en vers réguliers'. The oral tradition is apparently not
dead yet! It would also appear that Léon is not the only one
to make up stories to pass the time – he is also surrounded by
those of the other passengers.

However, it is the evocation of Léon's dream which owes
most to Virgil's epic. This dream is a synthesis of many
fragments of cultural knowledge and much of the day's
reflections, but its general conception and structure are inspired largely by Aeneas's visit to the Underworld in Book
Six of the *Aeneid*.

In both the *Aeneid* and Léon's dream the protagonist is
brought face to face with a reproachful Cumaean sibyl. It is
fitting that whereas in the *Aeneid*, the sibyl condemns Aeneas

[16] *The Works of the Emperor Julian,* translated by Wilmer Cave Wright,
3 vols, London: Heinemann, 1913, II, pp. 55, 57.

for not praying to the gods, in *La Modification* Léon's failing is his lack of self-awareness. It is also fitting that Léon is refused the protective golden bough to which Aeneas's mother guides him. Léon can expect no such divine help. His talisman is the book which he has taken with him but not opened and which prefigures the solution he will find in art. The sibyl in *La Modification* also informs Léon that he is coming in search of his father. While in the *Aeneid,* the protagonist finds his real father Anchises in the Underworld, Léon comes face to face with the father of the Catholic church – the Pope. However, the Pope's message is not what one would expect, suggesting as it does that Christian Rome is but a continuation of the Roman Empire (p. 261). Besides, Léon's 'real' father is, of course, the author of the book we are reading, and though Léon does not come face to face with him, he is made to confront his own authorial vocation. [17]

This vocation is also prefigured by the shower of paper which falls on him as he is ferried across the Styx by Charon (p. 224), an episode which may be an echo of the description in Book Three of the sibyl's leaves:

> She commits words to writing by making marks on leaves; afterwards she sorts into order all the prophecies which she has written on them, and allows their messages to remain, a closed secret, in her cave... if... as light wind strikes them, the delicate leaves are disturbed... and the prophetess never afterwards thinks of catching them as they flit within the rock-hollow. [18]

Léon will commit himself to leaves of paper and, like the sibyl, his subject-matter will be an enigma: 'cette énigme que

---

[17] Compare Joyce's Stephen Dedalus of whom Butor says 'Stephen Dedalus, le fils perpétuel, semble avoir rompu avec toute son ascendance intellectuelle, l'Eglise.... Ainsi, c'est autour du problème central des rapports entre père et fils, que se soue toute la dialectique d'*Ulysse*' (*8,* pp. 256, 258).

[18] Virgil, *The Aeneid,* translated by W. F. Jackson Knight, Harmondsworth: Penguin, 1956, p. 88.

désigne dans notre conscience ou notre inconscience le nom de Rome' (p. 276).

Butor's choice of Virgil is highly calculated. It may be a coincidence that both Butor and Virgil studied philosophy before turning to poetry, but it is no coincidence that Butor is borrowing from Rome's national epic, a work written to celebrate the origin and growth of the Roman Empire. There is also the obvious similarity in the facts that both are structured around a crucial journey and that both Aeneas and Léon abandon the women with whom they have been having an illicit affair (Dido and Cécile). But perhaps the most important similarity is a common didacticism. In both books the gods urge the protagonist to be true – Aeneas is told to be loyal to the gods, to his homeland, family and friends. Léon's visit to the psychological underworld of the dream is crucial to his realisation of where authenticity lies for him. In order to be loyal to himself Léon does not need to be unfaithful. Authenticity does not lie with another woman, but in the attempt to reconcile, in art, the different aspects of his culture. In this context it is interesting and important that Virgil – like the sibyls whom we shall shortly consider – was to be assimilated into Christian art. He was seen as a prophet of Christianity by Dante who made him his guide first to the Underworld and finally to the gates of Paradise.

MICHELANGELO

However, the most important cultural point of reference in *La Modification* is the work of Michelangelo. Michelangelo was an obvious choice for several reasons. *La Modification,* like all *nouveaux romans,* is to a very great extent concerned with the process of artistic creation. Léon is a future author and a representative of the novelist within the text. Michelangelo is the supreme representative of art, accomplished not in one but several media. Léon's plans are, of course, a lot less ambitious, but if the book we are reading corresponds to the one Léon hopes to write, it will have a certain universal dimension. For in his collage of memories and impressions Butor has taken care to include representatives of every generation (children, young lovers, the middle-aged couple, the widow, the old couple). The various seasons have been mentioned in the context of Léon's journeys. Night, day, dawn, dusk – all of them important motifs in Michelangelo's art – have been referred to. And, of course, historical and geographical references proliferate. It is surely no accident that the narrator comes back repeatedly to Bernini's *Fountain of the Four Rivers* representing the Nile, Ganges, Danube and the Río de la Plata, which were themselves metonyms for the continents of Africa, Asia, Europe and the Americas. Like Michelangelo in the *Last Judgement,* he even ventures into the underworld, though here it has become a metaphor for Léon's subconscious.

Michelangelo was also an apt choice of cultural reference given his role as an innovator. He not only reworked traditional forms in a highly self-conscious way but he also shocked his contemporaries by the new perspective which he offered on sacrosanct subjects such as the Last Judgement. The *nouveau roman* is by definition a self-conscious art form which at once plays with and defies traditional criteria and which has aroused a great deal of controversy.

Thirdly, both Michelangelo and Butor show an acute interest in the human body in motion. The Renaissance master rejected the traditional static and hieratic forms of religious painting, introduced a new dynamism and physicality into the treatment of sacred subjects and explored in them a wide range of movements and gestures. *La Modification* is punctuated by extremely detailed descriptions of the most banal movements, poses and gestures: the movements involved in the simple action of crossing one's legs (p. 26), the fidgeting of a fellow-passenger (pp. 20-21), the facial movements of another passenger (p. 199). The gesture rarely tells us anything specific about the character concerned. Often it seems to be included primarily for its graphic effect: 'vous avez vu les cheveux autrefois noirs d'Henriette, et son dos se détachant devant la première lumière terne et décourageante, doucement, brusquement au travers de sa chemise de nuit blanche un peu transparente' (p. 16). Like Claude Simon, Butor seems to be attempting to find a vocabulary precise enough to rival the painter's description of gesture and motion – an ambition dictated by a phenomenological interest in the human body in space and by a desire to suggest the complexity of movements which we rarely notice.

Fourthly and most importantly as far as Léon is concerned, Michelangelo's art is essentially a synthesis of Classical form and Christian ideology. This synthesis represents the ideal to which Léon must aspire if he is to achieve an equilibrium in his life. For neither Michelangelo nor Léon is the creation of a balance straightforward; their efforts are reflected in the writhing figures of Michelangelo's frescoes and sculptures and Léon's agonising and tortuous voyage of discovery. Indeed, Léon's physical discomfort – a counterpart to his mental anguish – is described in terms which may well be an echo of Michelangelo's *Brazen Serpent* which occupies one of the spandrels of the Sistine Chapel ceiling: 'Vous ne voulez pas vous retourner: vous avez peur de sentir l'haleine de cette gueule, de voir ce regard impitoyable et vitreux, les écailles de ce serpent épineux dont la queue froide s'enroule autour de vos jambes qui n'arrivent plus à se séparer' (p. 218).

Nowhere is this effort to synthesise more obvious then in the inclusion in the novel of a number of references to the sibyls and prophets which frame the principal scenes of the Sistine Chapel ceiling. Traditionally, the sibyls were seen as representatives of non-Jewish prophecy in whose cryptic messages could be read the coming of Christ. Michelangelo's juxtaposition of Classical and Old Testament prophets in this the Pope's chapel epitomises his efforts to combine Classical and Christian elements. In *La Modification,* Léon alludes explicitly to both the Persian (p. 192) and Cumaean sibyls (p. 171), the latter being the sibylline representative of Rome. Butor plays humorously on this theme of the prophecy or inscrutable message in a number of places, turning the inaudible announcements of railway loudspeakers into a banal modern equivalent (p. 47). The Old Testament prophets Ezekiel and Zachariah also figure in Léon's scheme of cultural references. Along with the sibyls, they provide him with ready points of comparison in his description of his travelling companions. The recurrent reference to Zachariah is partic-

ularly interesting. In Michelangelo's scheme on the Sistine
Ceiling, Zachariah is painted over the doorway. In *La Modification* Léon nicknames Zachariah an old man standing in
the doorway of the compartment. More importantly, Zachariah is traditionally a prophet who predicted the building of a
new Jerusalem and a new Temple. *La Modification* also
looks forward – to the new balance Léon will establish in his
life. Furthermore, the solution that he finds to his dilemma –
the writing of a book – is anticipated by an implicit reference
to Michelangelo's sibyls and prophets with their enormous
books: 'Les immenses personnages penchés au-dessus de vous
murmuraient, leurs doigts tournant les pages de leurs énor-
mes livres' (p. 266). The spiritual message offered by sibyls
and prophets may have no direct relevance for the modern
post-Absurdism reader, but Butor has been able to turn these
representatives of past civilisations to thematic effect in a
nouveau roman. The *nouveau roman* does not reject past
codes but incorporates them into new thematic patterns
which make us consider them in a new light and forces us to
recognise the absence of an absolute relationship between
meaning and symbol.

Michelangelo's work also acts as a catalyst for Léon's
realisation of the limitations of his relationship with Cécile.
In this relationship Léon has tried to ignore the moral dimension, to keep judgement at bay. However, the obsessional
reappearance of the *Last Judgement* in his consciousness
suggests that his Catholic conscience and sense of guilt cannot
be so easily repressed. Léon's attachment to his Catholic
culture emerges in particular in his dreams and certain
moments of near-hallucination between waking and sleep.
These are peppered with memories of the *Last Judgement*.
The description of Léon's sensation of floating is clearly a
reference to the distinctive depiction of the rising of the dead
in Michelangelo's painting: 'Vous sentiez que vos pieds ne
vous supportaient plus, qu'ils n'étaient même plus appliqués
sur le sol, qu'ils s'élevaient graduellement, que tout votre
corps pivotait dans l'espace jusqu'à se maintenir à la hauteur
des yeux fermés des gens assis' (pp. 257-58). By page 272
Léon has in his dream been found wanting in self-knowledge

and finds himself in a situation very reminiscent not only of
that of the damned in Michelangelo's *Last Judgement* but
also of the fate of the sinners in *Zachariah* and *Revelations*:

> C'est une foule de visages qui s'approchent, énormes et hain-
> eux comme si vous étiez un insecte retourné, des éclairs
> zébrant leurs faces et la peau en tombant par plaques.
> Votre corps s'est enfoncé dans la terre humide. Le ciel
> au-dessus de vous s'est mis à se zébrer d'éclairs, tandis que
> tombent de grandes plaques de boue qui vous recouvrent.
> (p. 272)

> And this shall be the plague wherewith the LORD will smite all
> the people that they have fought against Jerusalem: their flesh
> shall consume away while they stand upon their feet, and
> their eyes shall consume away in their holes, and their tongue
> shall consume away in their mouth.
> And it shall come to pass in that day, that a great tumult
> from the LORD shall be among them; and they shall lay hold
> every one on the hand of his neighbour, and his hand shall rise
> up against the hand of his neighbour. (*Zachariah* 14. 12-13)

This implicit identification with the damned was anticipated
some one hundred and fifty pages earlier in a reference to a
photograph of the *Last Judgement* representing 'un des
damnés cherchant à se cacher les yeux, au-dessus de la place
qui est restée vide jusqu'à Paris' (p. 99). It is no accident that
this reference comes immediately after a rather tense conversation with Cécile where Léon's bad conscience regarding the
situation was only too apparent.

It is clear from the foregoing discussion that the Michelangelo motif serves a number of functions in the text. Far
from being a gratuitous display of erudition, it is carefully
integrated into the thematic development of the novel and is
a crucial element in the evocation of Léon's growth in
awareness. Léon's attempt to chart Michelangelo's career
through Rome's art treasures is partly responsible for his
realisation that he should turn to writing and illustrates very
clearly a point made Butor about the way he himself perceives the world and approaches his work: 'Les peintres

m'enseignent à voir, à lire, à composer, donc à écrire, à disposer des signes dans une page' (*11*, p. 177). In the light of this statement it is fitting and significant that the promising dawn which greets Léon when he opens his eyes at the end of the novel is described in terms of a painting: 'Un des voyageurs ayant dévoilé la vitre entière, à un détour de la voie le soleil y a plongé ses pinceaux de cuivre, couvrant de minces plaques de métal chaud et lumineux les joues et les fronts des dormeurs' (p. 267).

Butor's interest in cultural codes places him squarely within the Structuralist generation. For Butor, as for Barthes, man –no matter how primitive, how ancient – is a creature with a culture. One of the things which interest him about Chateaubriand is the fact that at whatever nation Chateaubriand looks he finds a whole mythological, religious and cultural tradition. What Chateaubriand had happened upon – long before Barthes and Lévi-Strauss – is a 'constante de la nature humaine'. Cultural tradition is one of man's defining characteristics, but as we have already seen, we should be wary of confusing culture with truth. Cultural tradition is a universal human feature but individual traditions are relative both geographically and historically and twentieth-century man, as Butor conceives of him, will not find any absolute truth in Gallic, Classical or Christian culture. For Butor, the culture of the past surrounds us but does not provide eternally valid answers. Every age exposes flaws in the systems of previous ages: 'La bibliothèque nous donne le monde, mais elle nous donne un monde faux, de temps en temps des fissures se produisent' (*10*, p. 9). *La Modification* is driving a wedge into one such fissure.

4

Structure

CHANGES

La Modification is, as we have seen, part of a long tradition of journey-stories where physical displacement reflects the stages of a moral and psychological journey. Viewed as a journey, the fiction is governed by a strong forward impetus which is reinforced by Léon's own impression that his feelings are being determined by some mechanism outside of himself, a kind of fate (pp. 18-19, 21, 121, 224-25, 236-37, 265).

Furthermore our attention is drawn repeatedly to the concrete effects of time passing on the immediate surroundings. This is not simply the story of a change of mind – the modifications are multiple. Scrupulous attention is paid to the changes in the light conditions as the day proceeds, while inside the carriage time passing is signalled by the accumulation of debris on the floor, the gradual soiling of Léon's clothes, the growth of his beard. These trivial modifications are part of a network of variations on the theme 'modification' which relativises the major emotional shift. Thus, Cécile undergoes a metamorphosis when she goes to Paris with Léon (pp. 151-52); Henriette is said to have changed since her marriage (p. 177); Cécile aspires to transform Léon into a man, something, she says, Henriette has been unable to do (p. 179). By placing Léon's emotional crisis in a broader context of change, they anticipate and echo Léon's ultimate realisation that his mental 'fissure' is an aspect of a much more general phenomenon. In seeking to establish a relationship with Cécile, Léon was trying to recapture his youth. However, neither he nor his plans can escape the ravages of time: 'cette décision qui s'est peu à peu fanée, calcinée au cours du trajet, que vous ne parvenez plus à reconnaître, qui continue à se transformer sans que vous parveniez à freiner cette hideuse déliquescence' (pp. 208-09).

TIME AND SPACE: THE JOURNEY

Time is, however, not simply viewed as a process of ageing and decay. As a post-modernist writer, Butor is constantly drawing attention to the relativity of the ways in which we perceive and measure time. The novel starts with a discrepancy between the station clock and Léon's watch (p. 12) which suggests the fallibility of any time-measuring device. Similarly, no representation of time is ever definitive. The train timetable, one representation of the relationship between time and space, is condemned to dating (p. 29). Finally the perception of time is bound up with one's personal situation. Thus in the text Léon sets up a contrast between his own way of perceiving time and that of the newly-weds who, unlike him, are not counting the minutes before meeting a loved one:

> ... ils ont tant de choses à se dire, qu'ils n'ont pas besoin de faire durer les divers épisodes de ce voyage afin d'en combler autant que possible les vides et l'ennui, de ralentir le mouvement de leurs mâchoires comme vous tout à l'heure afin de ronger un peu plus de minutes, parce que n'importe quoi leur demandera beaucoup de temps et ne passera pour eux que trop vite... (p. 27)

The perception of space is also conditioned by a number of factors. In this age of travel and information, Butor argues, we are never simply in one place – we see that place through a grid of memories and information about other places. In all of Butor's novels any place is always the point of convergence of allusions to and associations with other places and times. Every place is the 'foyer d'un horizon d'autres lieux' (*11*, p. 57). Thus in *L'Emploi du temps*, through its street names, its geographical films, its art treasures, Bleston is the focal point of time- and space-spanning references. Similarly, in *La Modification* Léon's journey is punctuated by places which are rich in historical and cultural associations such as Fontainebleau with its legend of the Grand Veneur or Alise-Sainte-Reine where Julius Caesar beat the Gauls (p. 48). The novel is full of buildings and objects which have associations with other places – the travel agency opposite Léon's office with its exotic displays, the railway station with its destination-board, the plaque on the side of the train signalling the stopping-points, the train-compartment with its photographs of Paris, Rome, mountains and seascapes, the English and Italian newspapers read by the passengers (pp. 47, 92).

More significantly, whether Léon is in Paris or Rome, he cannot get away from reminders of the other city. Cecile's room in Rome is decorated with pictures of Paris; Léon's house in Paris is full of reminders of Rome and looks out on to the Panthéon. The two cities have been the cultural centres of the Western World and as such figure prominently in the European mentality. Bringing Cécile to Paris would not resolve the polarity. Thus, Léon sees his literary task in part as an exploration of the relationship between these two cities, of the way in which acquaintance with the one will colour the perception of the other:

> Il faudrait montrer dans ce livre le rôle que peut jouer Rome dans la vie d'un homme à Paris; on pourrait imaginer ces deux villes superposées l'une à l'autre... de telle sorte que toute localisation serait double, l'espace romain déformant plus ou moins pour chacun l'espace parisien, autorisant rencontres ou induisant en pièges. (p. 280)

For Butor, involuntary memory is an important part of our perception and the novel is full of Proustian moments. As in Proust, the conscious attempt to reconstruct the past is inadequate – Léon tries in vain to remember the layout of certain exhibits in the Louvre (p. 70). Yet an insignificant detail may have extraordinary power – just opening the lid of his case brings back forcefully domestic memories of that morning (pp. 24-25). In Rome Léon can scarcely take a step without being reminded of Cécile and their common past: 'chaque pierre presque, chaque mur de brique vous rappellera quelque parole de Cécile, quelque chose que vous avez lue ou apprise pour pouvoir lui en faire part' (p. 86). In the midst of these associations, however, Henriette retains one stronghold in Léon's memory – the Hôtel Quirinal where she and Léon spent their honeymoon and where, significantly, he continues to board on his trips to Rome.

However, it is the train journey which is the most important source of reminders of the other periods of his life. Françoise van Rossum-Guyon has identified references to ten journeys between Rome and Paris which are superimposed on one another in the narrative (*37*, p. 195). The narrative is thus constantly shifting between different periods of Léon's life, these shifts being effected largely through details in his surroundings which remind him of previous journeys. Fragments of the same journeys are evoked again and again, but it is only after they have been recounted several times that the truth emerges and that we see that all has not been bliss in the relationship with Cécile. Certain places along the route are invested with quite specific emotional reverberations. Thus Fontainebleau is associated in his mind with disappointment – after the two abortive trips with Cécile and Henriette to Paris and Rome – and anxiety about the future which is expressed in the obsessive repetition of the Grand Veneur's questions.

The narration of the current journey is, then, constantly being interrupted by cross-currents of memories and associations, where every instant or detail is the 'point d'origine et de convergence de plusieurs suites narratives': 'La narration n'est plus une ligne, mais une surface dans laquelle nous isolons un certain nombre de lignes, de points, ou de groupements remarquables' (*11*, p. 115). Subjective human time cannot be reduced to a linear sequence of chronologically or causally related events; the story of one individual's experience begs questions about the experience of his companions; the description of one place automatically involves allusion to several others.

The journey acts as a pivotal axis around which are arranged a number of crucial thematic paradoxes. In the course of the novel the inexorable objective chronology of the journey is relativised by the polydimensional nature of experienced, rememorative time and the closed space of the railway carriage is revealed to be the point of convergence for a host of references to other points in space. What starts out as a pilgrimage, a direct journey to a known destination turns out to be a quite awesome quest for truth which, it is recognised, will never be completed. The attempt to escape the familiar domestic scene turns paradoxically into a re-examination of the familiar and an attempt to understand Léon's place in it. And at the end of the day the tangible physical shift involved in a journey is irrelevant since Cécile will not even know that he has made the trip; what is important is the mental and spiritual journey he has made during that same period.

TRIPTYCH

The distance covered by Léon in the course of his spiritual journey is conveyed to a large extent through the interaction of the three sections of the novel, another feature which relativises the linearity of the text and reinforces Butor's insistence on the mobility of the novel form:

> Le micro-film est... un retour à la forme archaïque du rouleau, il nous oblige à lire le livre dans sa successivité. Le livre moderne, formé de feuilles superposées, s'est constitué pour permettre une liberté beaucoup plus grande dans la recherche à l'intérieur du texte. (*10,* p. 401)

The first section of the novel is dominated by Léon's dissatisfaction with Henriette and pleasure in the company of Cécile. A straightforward negative/positive opposition is set up between the two women. In this section there is a neat inversion of Christian values whereby Cécile is seen as his salvation (pp. 39-40), while Henriette is compared to a 'damnée' dragging him down with her to Hell: 'le morose plaisir des damnés à entraîner quelqu'un d'autre qu'eux dans leur marécage de poix et d'ennui' (p. 81). Generally, this section looks forward to a new life of freedom and romance with Cécile, and Léon lingers over memories of the first encounter with Cécile and his hopes for the immediate future (i.e. ignoring much of what has intervened). The data are presented as relatively simple and clear-cut; the decision is apparently made once and for all:

> Maintenant Cécile allait venir à Paris et vous demeureriez ensemble. Il n'y aurait pas de divorce, pas d'esclandre, de cela vous étiez, vous êtes bien certain; tout se passerait fort calmement, la pauvre Henriette se tairait, les enfants, vous iriez les voir une fois par semaine à peu près; et vous étiez certain aussi non seulement de l'accord, mais de la triomphante joie de Cécile qui vous avait tant taquiné sur votre bourgeoise hypocrisie. (p. 36)

In the second section the opposition between the two women is relativised. It emerges that when they met, they got on very well together, were able to bring out aspects of each other's personality of which Léon was ignorant. It also becomes clear that the relationship with Cécile does not run completely smoothly. Not only was the trip to Paris a failure, but in the much more recent past they have had a row because Léon broke his promise to have breakfast with Cécile – an omission which is symptomatic of his attitude to her in general: 'Mais vous lui aviez dit tant de choses la veille à mi-voix, et cela aussi vous l'aviez oublié' (p. 130). Furthermore, the tension caused by this thoughtlessness constitutes a nice echo to the disharmony referred to in the first section over Henriette's insistence on getting up to make breakfast for Léon before he leaves. The rosy picture initially presented by Léon is further qualified by one of the few extended speeches Cécile is allowed to make in the novel where it becomes clear that she is not fooled by his behaviour, that she has her own doubts about his sincerity (p. 140). The real gulf between them is highlighted by another argument on page 176. Here, typically, Léon tries to impose his own view by speaking for both of them, while Cécile maintains a distance agreeing with him in very cool, ironic terms. This gradual revelation of moments of disharmony is accompanied by a progressive qualification of the negative picture of Henriette given in the first part. On page 178, Léon is suspiciously ready to jump to her defence when he thinks Cécile is criticising her: 'Un monstre? Une pauvre femme malheureuse qui voudrait me faire couler avec elle dans son ennui'. This rather self-righteous remark constrasts sharply with his own hyperbolic and savage description of Henriette at the beginning of section two: 'cet énorme chancre insidieux qui recouvrait les traits d'Henriette d'un masque horrible se durcissant autour de sa bouche' (p. 106).

In this section too he speculates wistfully on what might have been, had his journey to Rome with Henriette taken place at a different time of the year (p. 148). Furthermore, he goes so far as to suggest that if it had not been for this failed reconciliation he might not love Cécile so much. The clear-cut distinction between the two relationships has crumbled. The success of the one may depend simply on the failure of the other – not a very solid foundation. In addition, through-out this section memories from the past interfere more and more with Léon's clear plans. The future becomes problem-atic and Léon begins to worry about living a lie with his family until he can settle with Cécile (p. 107). At one point he becomes so demoralised that he imagines a defeatist version of the future whereby he simply returns to Henriette (p. 133). The irritation with his wife and child which figured so prominently in the first section is now qualified by a desire to stay in touch with them. By the end of the section his doubts, qualifications and unresolved emotions have confused the issues and culminate in a crisis of defeatism which will undermine all his plans.

The third section forms a pendant to the first section. Léon's decision has disintegrated to the point where, on pages 274-75, he offers a perspective on the next few days which is a point by point negation of his initial plans. The attractive plot he had outlined is systematically undone:

Vous n'irez point guetter les volets de Cécile; vous ne la verrez point sortir; elle ne vous apercevra point.

Vous n'irez point l'attendre à la sortie du palais Farnèse; vous déjeunerez seul; tout au long de ces quelques jours, vous prendrez tous vos repas seul.

The relationship with Cécile has become a thing of the past rather than the future. Gradually unpleasant memories associated with Cécile occupy more and more space. Many of the features – reproaches, resentment, hostility – which marked his relationship with Henriette are attributed to the affair with Cécile, and he goes so far as to admit that if Cécile came to live in Paris, she would simply be another woman like all the rest (p. 278). On page 264 there is a nice echo of a scene from the first section which makes a similar point. Early in the first section Léon offered a little vignette of his cold farewell to his wife before setting out: 'Sur le palier, vous n'aviez pas osé lui refuser son baiser triste... Elle a refermé la porte de votre appartement avant que vous ayez commencé à descendre les marches, perdant ainsi sa dernière occasion de vous attendrir' (pp. 17-18). His leavetaking of Cécile, after their trip to Paris, is even more cold – here he is not even bound by the dutiful kiss of the spouse: 'Vous avez monté les valises de Cécile jusqu'à son palier, via Monte della Farina, puis vous l'avez quittée très vite sans l'embrasser, en lui murmurant seulement, comme par acquit de conscience: "Alors, à ce soir"' (p. 264).

At the same time the best period of his past with Henriette – the honeymoon – is recounted. The image of the life-denying and faded Henriette of the first half is displaced by that of the young, enthusiastic bride. The memory of his idyllic honeymoon also belies the statement in the first section to the effect that he never really loved Rome till he knew Cécile (p. 60). His relationship with her proves to be not nearly so unconventional and free as he thinks but is partly modelled on the early period of his marriage with Henriette and on the image of marital bliss he sees in the young couple on the train.

In the third section too the self-satisfaction Léon showed in the first part regarding his position and wealth – he was constantly drawing supercilious comparison between his own social status and that of his travelling companions – gives way to a more modest and relativistic realisation of his place in the general scheme of things. The book closes, as it opens, with plans for the future, but those plans are quite different. At the beginning of the book Léon was ready to throw himself into a physical relationship which would let him forget his family and responsibilities and the fact that he is ageing. At the end of the book his plans are much more constructive. Furthermore, his awareness of the power he wields professionally – a letter from him can make his subordinates fear for their jobs (p. 27) – has given way to the acknowledgement that, as a writer, he will never exhaust his subject. To reinforce this point, there is on page 276 an ironic reworking of the concept of divine grace. The facile opposition between the salvation offered by Cécile and the hell offered by Henriette is replaced by a recognition that 'je ne puis espérer me sauver seul', that he will have to look outside of himself to art and communication in his search for truth. By this time, of course, truth is seen as a much more problematical question and his recognition on page 274 that he will never be able to explain his change of mind to Cécile contrasts sharply with the naivety of his declaration at the beginning of section two to the effect that he would tell Cécile everything he had been doing so that there would be no lies between them.

Finally, the experience through which he realises his vocation – the dream – is structurally crucial, drawing together and synthesising in a journey into the subconscious the thoughts and observations which have marked the physical journey in the course of the book. By recombining details from the other sections of the novel in a new mini-narrative which defies waking logical and causal explanations, Butor offers a new perspective on Léon's past, confirms that all is not as clear-cut as he once thought and gives a foretaste of the difficulty of the task he faces – if he is going to achieve any understanding of himself, Léon will have to try to unravel this intricate mental skein.

In *La Modification* as in his other novels, Butor has created a structure which is as complex and suggestive as the ideas with which he is dealing. Typical of Butor is the choice of a very restricted time-scale and a single locus as the principal temporal and spatial co-ordinates for the fiction. *Passage de Milan* records twenty-four hours in a Paris tenement, *L'Emploi du temps* a year in an English town; *Degrés* is an attempt to record an hour's lesson in a Parisian school. *La Modification* covers a night passed in a railway carriage. The apparent classical simplicity of these narrative situations is, however, quickly complicated in each text by the proliferation of personal and mythical associations, historical and geographical parallels which raise fundamental questions about both our own situations and the representations to which we are exposed. The most banal activity takes place in a cultural, historical and geographical context of quite bewildering complexity and any attempt to record it chronologically is intensely selective. The attempt in *Degrés* to give a full account of a single hour in a French classroom turns out to be an almost super-human enterprise as the protagonist delves further into the varied cultural baggage of the pupils which is constantly impinging on the way they and he view the world. And since, in Butor, every moment in time, every locus is a nucleus of references to other times and places, there is an acute tension in his novels between the classical unity of this overall macro-structure and the baroque intricacy and profusion of the micro-structure, between the apparent limits of the fictional situation – the class, the journey, the year abroad – and the boundless allusiveness of the text. In Butor's terms the active involvement of the reader in the text and the questions it raises depends on the paradoxical creation of a structure which is controlled and intricate but incomplete – a structure which suggests something of the cultural structures and parallels underpinning our experience but which does not exhaust them:

Pour qu'une œuvre soit vraiment inachevée... pour qu'elle
nous invite à la continuer, il faut qu'à certains égards elle soit
particulièrement soignée... Si nous avons seulement une es-
quisse un peu vague, elle ne comportera pas de lignes suffisamment fortes pour nous inciter à les prolonger; par contre,
la composition très puissante une fois brisée va me con-
traindre à la rétablir. (*10*, p. 19)

5

Self-Reflexivity and Technical Experimentation

T H E introductory remarks to this study established two fundamental constants in the *nouveau roman* – formal experimentations and self-reflexivity. In the pursuit of these features, Butor is one of the most moderate *nouveaux romanciers*. In comparison with Alain Robbe-Grillet, Butor seems much less inclined to flout verisimilitude, and on the whole his novels stay within the bounds of credibility even when they are at their most self-conscious. Like Gide in *Les Faux-Monnayeurs,* the principal means used by Butor to give thematic status to the process of writing is to include within the text a character who aspires to be a writer, who wishes through writing to come to an understanding of himself and confer some sort of significance on the reality around him. Both Butor and his protagonists are in one way or another engaged in a quest for truth – a quest which they recognise as being doomed to failure but which remains compulsive: 'Tout livre achevé, fermé, plein, est... un masque, une façade; le livre véritable, le livre juste est nécessairement lui-même ruine, délabrement découvreur' (*7,* p. 212). In *La Modification* Léon realises that he will never be able to get to the bottom of the attraction which Rome has for Western man. Yet he feels compelled to explore the question in a book in an attempt to understand the forces governing his own life (p. 239) and, even if he does not free himself from those forces, at least lay the foundations for a time when perhaps man will understand himself and his culture better: 'ce qu'il vous faudrait maintenant examiner à loisir et de sang-froid, c'est l'assise et le volume réel de ce mythe que Rome est pour vous... afin d'améliorer votre connaissance des liaisons qu'il a avec les conduites et décisions de vous-même' (p. 239), 'Donc préparer, permettre, par exemple au moyen d'un livre, à cette liberté future hors de notre portée, lui permettre, dans une mesure si infime soit-elle de se constituer' (p. 276).

The decision to change one's lifestyle is not enough. Freedom will depend on a truthful re-examination of one's past, an examination which will try to eliminate the illusions and obscurity which dogged it:

> Une conversion n'est pas suffisante; il ne s'agit pas seulement de prendre la décision d'orienter son avenir dans une direction différente de celle qu'il semblait devoir suivre, mais il faut aussi faire de son passé autre chose que ce qu'il demeurerait inévitablement si on le laissait en paix, une source d'obscurités et d'erreurs, la série confuse et opaque des expériences d'un de ces individus noyés dans une irresponsable foule, autre chose, c'est-à-dire une source de connaissance; il faut en extraire tout l'enseignement. (*8*, p. 362)

The past has lessons to teach for the future – Léon's relationships with both women have been marked by deception and self-deception and there can be neither truth nor any measure of free will until he has acknowledged his mistakes. The full extent of Léon's modification can be measured if one compares these conclusions with his attitude at the beginning of the novel. There, Rome was seen as a place of authenticity and oblivion – a telling juxtaposition in Léon's mind. There, the terms in which he expressed himself suggested a tendency to look outside himself for some magical solution: 'cette magicienne qui par la grâce d'un seul de ses regards vous délivre de toute cette horrible caricature d'existence, vous rend à vous-même dans un bienfaisant oubli de ces meubles, de ces repas, de ce corps tôt fané, de cette famille harassante' (p. 40). By page 240 he has realised that a serious attempt to find the truth is a much more difficult enterprise. Here even in sleep he cannot find oblivion – his dreams are signs which have to be read with considerable effort: 'vous restituant vous-même à cette tranquille terreur, à cette émotion primitive où s'affirme avec tant de puissance et de hauteur, au-dessus des ruines de tant de mensonges, la passion de l'existence et de la vérité' (p. 240). The full difficulty of telling the truth is brought home forcefully to Léon a couple of pages later when he tries to think of a way in which to break off the relationship with Cécile and realises the extent to which human emotion and contextual factors affect truth and its perception: 'Toutes les circonstances, tous vos actes des jours précédents lui paraîtront vous démentir; elle ne pourra pas vous croire; elle verra dans tout cela de la grandeur d'âme' (p. 242). By the end of the journey he has realised that Cécile is not his solution. There is no such easy answer, as is indicated by the fact that he is refused the Golden Bough in his dream. His true salvation lies in the effort of writing.

However, Butor and his protagonists are not only looking for truth – they are also seeking to put some order into their lives, to give some meaning and structure to their experiences. Again and again in his criticism, Butor argues that writing is a kind of 'colonne vertébrale': 'il est ainsi un prodigieux moyen de se tenir debout, de continuer à vivre intelligemment à l'intérieur d'un monde quasi furieux qui vous assaille de toutes parts' (*11*, p. 17). Throughout Léon's journey, he has been haunted by a multitude of memories, 'veillé par tant d'images, incapable de les ordonner et de les nommer' (p. 261). In the flux of experience and memory, writing represents a way of avoiding disintegration, a way of consolidating 'tout le sable de [ses] jours' (p. 276).

By the end of his journey Léon is beginning to glimpse some of the fundamental principles governing his life. The analogies which he concocts between his own situation and the couples on the train put his relationship with Henriette in the more general context of the ages of man. He and Henriette represent the middle-aged couple – they are the natural mid-point between the honeymooners and the old couple. Viewed in this light, the relationship with Cécile is an attempt to avoid the inevitable. Secondly, he comes to realise that beyond the superficial question of the relative attractiveness of two women, there is a more fundamental and more general question concerning the multiple factors which deter-

mine the decisions we make – culture, codes, symbols, inclina-
tions, free will. Léon's initial decision was based on the
assumption that he was a free agent with full responsibility
for his decisions. This journey – by removing him physically
from the immediate context of either relationship – suspends
such assumptions, gives him an insight into the issues at stake
in any decision.

In 'Le Roman et la poésie', Butor identifies a third
attribute of the novelist. He is able to read the signs around
him: 'Le romancier est alors celui qui aperçoit que les choses
autour de lui commencent à mumurer, qui va mener ce
murmure jusqu'à la parole' (*11,* p. 47). Léon shows such a
tendency in the acute attention he pays to the luggage and
belongings of the other passengers and the hypotheses which
he forms on the basis of that evidence. The most banal
objects are a sign. Nationality can be identified from the sort
of clothes worn by the characters (pp. 92, 168), passport
colour (p. 158), newspapers (pp. 47, 92). Léon's suitcase is so
representative of his life that it can serve as a kind of
exposition. A description of it at the beginning of the novel
gives the reader the essential information, suggesting not only
a discrepancy between his self-importance and a certain
shabbiness but also the extent to which his life is based on
illusion:

> ...votre propre valise recouverte de cuir... avec vos initiales
> frappées 'LD', cadeau de votre famille à votre précédent
> anniversaire, qui était alors assez élégante, tout à fait convena-
> ble pour le directer du bureau parisien des machines à écrire
> Scabelli, et qui peut encore faire illusion malgré ces taches
> grasses qui se révèlent à un examen plus attentif... (p. 10)

Here, as in his essay on fashion 'Mode et moderne' (*12,*
pp. 399-414), the influence of the structuralist critic Roland
Barthes is evident. For both Butor and Barthes, the world is
saturated with sign-systems. We are surrounded by objects
which – irrespective of their banality – contain a message:
'cette serviette noire... au-dessus de lui comme un emblème,
comme une légende qui n'en est pas moins explicative, ou

énigmatique, pour étre une chose, une possession et non un mot' (p. 8).

Finally, Butor argues that the novelist in his formal research should provide a key to the way in which the novel is composed. For Butor, the novel is by definition self-reflexive: 'Le roman tend tout naturellement et il doit tendre à sa propre élucidation' (*11*, p. 13). Thus, in *La Modification,* Léon does not restrict himself to idle speculation about the belongings of the other passengers. On the contrary, he is constantly embarking on imaginative versions of their entire lives. There is scarcely a passenger for whom Léon does not make up a story. On page 193 he gives a highly compressed account of what he imagines may be the main co-ordinates in the lives of the old couple: 'il a peut-être été professeur ou employé dans une banque. Ils ont dû avoir des enfants. Ils ont perdu un fils à la guerre. Ils vont au baptême d'une petite-fille. Ils n'ont pas l'habitude de voyager'. Elsewhere, his narratives are much more ornate – he recounts in considerable imaginary detail the girlhood of 'Madame Polliat' (pp. 125-26), the love-story of 'Pierre' and 'Agnès' (pp. 136-37), the dramatic domestic background of the two adolescent boys (pp. 156-57), the inner troubles of the priest (pp. 87-88). The urge to compose stories is very strong in Léon. Even pictorial representations around him seem to beg questions about what preceded and followed: 'Vous en contempliez les personnages si naïvement peints qu'ils invitent l'esprit à leur insuffler la vie, de sorte que vous en êtes arrivé à imaginer pour chacun d'eux une histoire, les suivant avant et après la scène repré-sentée' (p. 70).

In all of these examples Butor is very clearly giving prominence to the activity of creating narratives and, in the fictional lives of the minor characters, he is making it clear that the fiction is not a slavish representation of reality – the source of a fiction may be remarkably tenuous and there is no one-to-one correspondence between language and repre-sentation. The fiction is an experimental ground and stories are not only composed but can also be undone. This is what happens in the case of 'Madame Polliat', whose story is systematically 'undone' on pages 138-39: 'Vous ne pouvez

pas voir le petit garçon à côté d'elle qui n'est peut-être pas
son neveu; elle n'est peut-être pas veuve, elle ne s'appelle pas
Madame Polliat, et il y a bien peu de chance pour que son
prénom soit André'. Butor also draws attention to the freedom of the author in the whimsical way in which Léon plays
with proper names, applying them to and taking them away
from characters at will. One minute he is calling the little boy
Thomas after his son; shortly afterwards he has decided to
call him André. The name André itself is attributed to more
than one character: 'ce n'est plus à Henri... ou à son frère...
que vous pourriez appeler André maintenant que le neveu de
la veuve est sorti et que ce prénom reste libre' (p. 156). On
pages 168-69, Léon applies to a single character a whole
gamut of different names based on a single syllable glimpsed
in a passport.

Nowhere is the gap between representational fiction and
self-reflexive fiction more obvious than in this play on
names. Traditionally, the proper name was the exclusive
attribute of a single character. It frequently told the reader
something about the character; at the very least it provided a
shorthand way of referring to a character and immediately
conjured up a certain combination of attributes and motives.
In the post-modernist novel, the assumed one-to-one relationship between name and character has been undermined.
Already in Proust, the name is a catalyst for reverie and
speculation on the part of the narrator who may attach to it a
multitude of associations and qualities which are quite re-
mote from the character referred to. Far from being an
economical and clarificatory form of shorthand, it may generate in the narrator's imagination numerous mini-narratives.
In Faulkner, the attribution of the same name to different
characters confuses rather than aids the reader and demands
of him a much more active effort of understanding. In the
nouveau roman, even when writers do not actively disrupt
the coherence of the narrative, as in Butor's case, they are
nevertheless keen to remind us of the purely fictitious nature
of what we are reading. Léon's experiments with various
names produce new combinations of backgrounds and cir-

cumstances and thereby suggest the way in which Butor must have proceeded in the making of his narrative.

MISE EN ABYME

The *mise en abyme* has come to represent the hallmark of the *nouveau roman*. The concept itself is not new and can be traced back to André Gide's *Journal*.[19] Gide uses the term to describe the sort of mirror effect which one gets when there is included within a text or within a painting a passage or an object (often in the form of a representation within a representation) which takes up and presents in miniature one of the main themes of the work: 'J'aime assez qu'en une œuvre d'art, on retrouve ainsi transposé à l'échelle des personnages, le sujet même de cette œuvre. Rien ne l'éclaire et n'établit plus sûrement les proportions de l'ensemble'. He uses the examples of the sub-play in Hamlet and the little mirrors which one finds in Flemish painting where the main scene is often reflected in a mirror on a back wall, the wittier even including the reflection of the painter at work. In his own critical writings, Butor has drawn attention to a similar phenomenon in the imaginary works of art described in Proust's *A la recherche du temps perdu,* which encapsulate some of the major themes and highlight the compositional method of the work: 'à travers [certaines œuvres d'Elstir et de Vinteuil] Proust prend peu à peu conscience du développement de son propre travail... elles sont des modes de sa réflexion créatrice' (*8,* p. 130).

Undoubtedly, the clearest example of a *mise en abyme* in *La Modification* is the description of the likely content of the book which Léon bought for the journey (pp. 197-98). Léon reckons that this is probably the evocation of a journey of self-discovery and as such it obviously echoes his own situation and the novel we are reading. The reference to the unrecognisable photograph on his *carte d'identité* (p. 53) is another *mise en abyme* reflecting Léon's inability to recog-

---

[19] André Gide, *Journal: 1889-1936,* Paris: Gallimard, 1948, p. 41.

nise himself or acknowledge his most fundamental desires. Furthermore, in the same wallet there are his 'carte de la Société des amis du Louvre' and 'celle de la Société Dante Alighieri' which could be seen as an image of the divided life he leads. This latter theme is also alluded to in the discreet reference to the reproduction of 'l'allégorie des deux amours à la villa Borghese'.

Many of the *mises en abyme* have a more general application to the novel form. The emphatically recurrent references to Bernini's fountain draw attention to the universal dimension of the work of art, its capacity to span the world through its range of references. This point is also made by the display in the travel agency window with its proliferation of references to exotic places and other cultures (pp. 62-63) or the train-timetable with its advertisements from a multitude of places along the line (p. 26). This grand conception of the universality of the work of art is common to all of Butor's fiction, which incorporates references to a remarkable range of places and periods, and, of course, the journey is a particularly rich field of allusion:

> Les lieux ayant toujours une historicité soit par rapport à l'histoire universelle, soit par rapport à la biographie de l'individu, tout déplacement dans l'espace impliquera une réorganisation de la structure temporelle, changements dans les souvenirs et dans les projets, dans ce qui vient au premier plan, plus ou moins profond et plus ou moins grave. (*11*, pp. 120-21)

The *mise en abyme* can also serve as a warning to the reader against misreadings. The description on page 49 of the way in which the university lecturer is flicking through his text looking for the 'important' quotation is a good example of the wrong way to approach a *nouveau roman*. In the *nouveau roman* the old distinction between the important and the banal has been undermined. The interest of the *nouveau roman* does not depend on a lively plot organised around monumental events. Writers like Butor and Claude Simon are more interested in those areas of experience which we take for granted, which are not given explicit coverage in the traditional novel. Another warning is given on page 284 in the reference to Léon's *guide bleu* which has become outdated over the years. As Jacques Revel found out in *L'Emploi du temps,* any attempt to document the world is condemned to obsolescence. The world is constantly changing, constantly devaluing the representation. The most the writer can hope to do is to provide a new structure through which we can view the world. He can never have the last word.

NARRATIVE POINT OF VIEW

Undoubtedly the most immediately striking feature of *La Modification* and one which signals it as an experimental novel is its use of the second person plural pronoun throughout. The first word of the text is 'vous' and arrests the reader's attention with such force that it surely demands a qualification of Butor's own rashly absolute commentary on Joyce's *Ulysses*: 'Nul livre ne commence de façon plus abrupte' (*8,* p. 260). However, this is not simply an eye-catching trick. In the *nouveau roman* the reader does not simply passively receive a story. The *nouveau roman* spurns identification and the attempt to create an illusion in favour of a much more active appreciation of the technical questions of the novel. In the *nouveau roman* the reader is not allowed to forget that he is reading a text and in *La Modification* the use of the second person plural form serves as a constant reminder of the author-reader pact underlying all literature. Butor insists in his criticism that the author does not simply write for his own satisfaction. Contrary to what many would have us believe, the author, according to Butor, has his eye on his audience – he is always implicitly addressing the reader. In *La Modification,* Butor makes this address explicit:

> Cette réflexion qui se produit à l'intérieur du livre n'est que le commencement d'une réflexion publique qui va éclairer l'écrivain lui-méme. Il cherche... à donner... un sens à son

existence. Ce sens, il ne peut évidemment le donner tout seul; ce sens c'est la réponse même que trouve peu à peu parmi les hommes cette question qu'est un roman. (*11*, p. 29)

The use of the second person form is also closely related to Butor's didactic intention. Léon's story has a relevance for our own situation and begs many questions about our own culture and historical awareness. Léon is the link between reader and author – not only is he a reader himself but Butor argues that we are all aspiring novelists to some degree: 'Le romancier en titre est celui qui réussit à mener à son terme cette activité que nous esquissons tous, mais à laquelle, la plupart du temps, nous sommes forcés de renoncer, qui la poursuit pour nous' (*10*, p. 9). Considered in this light, Léon is a kind of intermediary figure, the 'vous' an intermediary form of narrative point of view which involves the reader linguistically in the recounting of Léon's story. Perhaps the clearest indication of this link between Butor's technique and his didacticism is to be found in Léon's fanciful variations on the type of composition titles which the schoolmaster-priest might set his pupils:

Imaginez que vous êtes monsieur Léon Delmont et que vous écrivez à votre maîtresse Cécile Darcella pour lui annoncer que vous avez trouvé pour elle une situation à Paris. (p. 115)

Imaginez que vous voulez vous séparer de votre femme; vous lui écrivez pour lui expliquer la situation. (ibid.)

Such instructions are crude exercises in story-making, but they force the addressee to look at the world from a different point of view. Unlike such schoolchildren, the reader of the *nouveau roman* is not being asked to suspend his critical distance and enter the skin of an imaginary character, but he is being asked to participate in the working out of a philosophical and perceptual problem which underlies the way in which we all view the world.

The 'vous' goes beyond Léon to address the reader and question his assumptions too. The novel for Butor is a means of investigation – a fact which also explains the notable number of questions punctuating the text. This interpretation is also corroborated by Butor himself in an illuminating commentary on the use of 'vous': 'C'est ainsi qu'un juge d'instruction ou un commissaire de police, dans un interrogatoire rassemblera les différents éléments de l'histoire que l'acteur principal ou le témoin ne peut ou ne veut lui raconter, et qu'il les organisera dans un récit, un discours à la seconde personne, qui sera par conséquent toujours un récit "didactique"' (*7*, p. 66). This interrogation/reconstruction procedure is particularly appropriate in a novel where the protagonist is so fundamentally unsure of himself. It allows Butor to suggest more about Léon than this latter knows himself and to demonstrate the process by which he comes to gain insight and an ability express himself: 'Nous sommes dans une situation d'enseignement: ce n'est plus seulement quelqu'un qui possède la parole comme un bien inaliénable, inamovible, comme une faculté innée qu'il se contente d'exercer, mais quelqu'un à qui l'on donne la parole' (*7*, p. 66). It is therefore not surprising that at the end of the novel Léon aims to write a book in which he will 'tenter de faire revivre sur le mode de la lecture cet épisode crucial de votre aventure, le mouvement qui s'est produit dans votre esprit' (pp. 285-86). The 'vous' form of narration is able to give the reader access both to information about the protagonist of which the protagonist is aware and information about him of which he is not aware.

However, the narrative data are not conveyed entirely and without exception in the second person plural form. In a number of places the first person pronoun intrudes very briefly. This is not to be attributed to careless inconsistency on Butor's part, for if one pays attention to the context it becomes clear that the 'je' appears at points in the narrative which are concerned with turning-points in Léon's life:

Il y a eu un grand pas de fait: j'ai réussi à ce qu'elle soit avec moi ailleurs que dans Rome... pendant tout ce séjour à Paris où d'ordinaire je souffre tant d'être loin d'elle... je saurai qu'elle est là, je pourrai la voir de temps en temps. (p. 142)

or where he is beginning to raise crucial questions about his
intentions, decisions, assumptions:

> Ah, non, cette décision que j'avais eu tant de mal à prendre,
> il ne faut pas la laisser se défaire ainsi; ne suis-je donc pas
> dans ce train, en route vers Cécile merveilleuse? (p. 162)

> tandis que moi... que ferai-je, à quel saint, quelle sainte me
> vouerai-je? (p. 191)

The very tight control which Butor keeps over the technique
and thematic development of his text allows him to register
key moments in Léon's life and in his growth in awareness in
an extremely discreet way. Léon may not have direct access
to the narration of his own story here, but he will in the book
he writes, and these brief incursions of the first person into
La Modification anticipate the time when he will be capable
of speaking in his own voice.

THE DREAM

On the level of experimentation, the other most striking
feature in Butor is his extensive use of dream sequences. *Le
Passage de Milan, L'Emploi du temps, Degrés* and *La Modification* all include quite lengthy descriptions of dreams,
while in his critical writings Butor took a dream of Baudelaire's as a starting point for the study of the poet (6). Butor's
recourse to dreams in his novels is very much in line with the
relativisation of the distinction between the real and the
imaginary, the verisimilitudinous and the fantastic carried
out by other *nouveaux romanciers,* in particular Robbe-
Grillet. In *La Modification,* Butor himself blurs this distinction in the latter part of the dream sequence where the
brackets initially enclosing dream material are eliminated and
there is no clear typographical signal that a dream sequence is
beginning or ending.

However, more important than this coincidence of interest with other *nouveaux romanciers* is the fact that Butor

is taking up the challenge posed to traditional novelistic psychology by Freudian theory and is exploring in a fairly systematic way areas of experience normally only touched on incidentally in novels. Butor argues in fact that the novel is the ideal form in which to consider both the most banal aspects of daily routine and the most irrational areas of human experience:

> Il n'y a pas pour le moment de forme littéraire dont le pouvoir soit aussi grand que celui du roman. On peut y relier d'une façon extrêmement précise, par sentiment ou par raison, les incidents en apparence les plus insignifiants de la vie quotidienne et les pensées, les intuitions, les rêves en apparence les plus éloignés du langage quotidien. (*11*, pp. 16-17)

The dream holds a particular interest for Butor the phenomenologist insofar as it is a state where rationality is temporarily suspended and the world is viewed in a new light. Dreams give access to a whole new universe which is the complement of everyday reality, but this universe is more fluid, is not subject to the same rules as reality. In the dream the hard contours of what we consider to be reality are questioned: 'par les fissures que l'attention décèle dans le réel, se révèle un univers complémentaire de la réalité durcie' (*39*, p. 81). In dreams banal data of the previous day's experience, memories and thoughts reflected upon in the course of the day, associations and sensory impressions are juxtaposed in unusual and defamiliarising combinations. It is impossible to examine here every stage in Léon's dreams in detail. They combine scenes and details which have their source in a variety of areas of human experience. There are the cultural memories of Christian art and literature, the *Aeneid*, Classical mythology and Gallic folklore. For instance, Léon's feeling that the floor is opening up below him – clearly an expression of doubt about his decision – owes a lot to the evocation of the Classical underworld and the Christian conception of Hell. There are personal memories of previous journeys, visits to Rome and Cécile's visit to Paris. The geological 'fossé' of his dream (p. 206) translates in concrete terms the metaphorical 'fossé qu'avait creusé entre vous le séjour parisien' (p. 225). Finally, many of the details of his dream are generated by details in his surroundings or by recent sensory impressions. The raindrops in the window, the moonlight, the nightlight, the book he is carrying, the noise of the train, the smell of smoke, the coolness of the window against his forehead all have an echo somewhere in his dream. The faceless figure which haunts the dream and which gives expression to the crucial question of identity underlying the novel turns out to have been partly inspired by someone in the railway compartment whose face has been hidden by shadow (p. 283).

Léon's dreams clearly make highly unorthodox narratives with no clear logical or psychological links between the different elements and their combinations. However, they do correspond to the principles whereby, Freud argued, 'dreams have no means at their disposal for representing... logical relationships between the dream thoughts'. [20] In both Butor's and Freud's analysis of the dream, logical relationships are replaced by simultaneity and the juxtaposition of the unlike. The dream in both combines the 'sources which have acted as stimuli for the dream into a single unity in the dream itself'. [21] The first incursion into Léon's dreams (pp. 201) provides an example of this process of condensation and combination. This dream draws on the myth of the Grand Veneur, the description of the Cumaean sibyl in the *Aeneid,* the memory of a passport check on the trip to Paris with Cécile and details from Léon's physical surroundings – the grille in the floor, the rain, the book he has taken with him. All of these elements are combined in a single mini-narrative which gives an unfamiliar perspective on the thoughts and sensations re-counted elsewhere and suggests that there may be a pattern to them which neither the reader nor Léon has identified yet.

In the dream the preoccupations of our waking hours may be partially eclipsed by things and ideas to which we normally

[20] *The Interpretation of Dreams,* translated by J. Strachey, edited by A. Richards, Harmondsworth: Pelican, 1976, p. 422.
[21] *The Interpretation of Dreams,* p. 266.

pay scant attention – the process which Freud calls displacement. Thus on pages 237-38 the act of asking for a glass of
wine in an Italian café – something Léon must have done on
countless occasions – becomes a highly dramatic and violent
scene in his dream. In this episode Léon's statement that he is
thirsty is at first ignored by the other people in the café and,
when he is reluctantly served, the bitter taste of the wine
causes him to shatter the glass in frustration. Though the
relationship between this scene and Léon's current, problematical situation is far from obvious, the transformation of
what should be a banal incident into a highly charged and
scandalous event suggests that we are touching on something
much more profound. This particular dream marks an important stage in the narrative insofar as it expresses Léon's
subconscious realisation that his fundamental needs cannot
be exhausted by the pagan side of Rome. Until now his
appreciation of Rome was superficial and facile, that of the
pleasure-seeker wining, dining and sightseeing. Henceforth,
he will have to go beyond the easy lifestyle, look at Rome
seriously, try to understand what it means to him on a
deeper, spiritual level. If dreams are fulfilled wishes as Freud
argues, then the smashing of the glass represents the desire to
reject his previous lifestyle.

The dream is, of course, one area where repressed and
censored thoughts and desires may manifest themselves. In
Butor too the dream is a means of access to the protagonist's
most deep-seated desires, desires of which he is often not
aware in his waking life. Before he falls asleep Léon imagines
that he will dream fondly about his new life with Cécile
(p. 127). In fact, ironically, the opposite is true – the dreams
simply confirm that this would not be the right decision and
point to desires of which he has not been aware. The parallel
descriptions of the processions of cardinals (p. 160) and
emperors (pp. 269-70), which are each followed by crucial
questions about his love of Rome, suggest a desire for a better
balance in his attitude to Rome. The dream fulfils this desire
in its fusion of the Christian Hell with the Classical Underworld, its combination of references to Christian and Classical art, Jesus Christ and Roman Gods. The repeated reference

to the two-headed Janus is undoubtedly the best embodiment of this desire for balance and the reconciliation of the two sides of Rome. Like Janus – aptly the god of new beginnings – Léon must try to look in two different directions at once without favouring one over the other.

An even more important element of his dreams is the recurrent reference to his inability to express himself. Again and again in his dreams the protagonist experiences problems either in articulating in language what he wants to say or in making himself understood by those around him (pp. 5, 250, 261). Furthermore, Léon, like the old man opposite him, talks in his sleep (p. 216) as if compelled to try to verbalise the unconscious. Léon's real desire is to express himself, but the only way he can do this is through writing. He knows he will not be able to explain himself to Cécile (p. 274). The spoken word is inadequate. He will have to resort to writing, will have to undertake the serious and difficult task of exploring his situation in a medium which has a more permanent and universal dimension than the transient conversation between romantically involved individuals.

Ultimately, then, the dream is another of the many narratives which surround us all the time and which help us process reality, whether that reality is the glut of data which impinges on our senses at every moment or whether it is repressed desires specific to the individual. Like those other narratives which condition our perception, it must be considered as an integral part of reality and taken into account in any attempt to represent it: 'Il ne peut y avoir de réalisme véritable que si l'on fait sa part à l'imagination, si l'on comprend que l'imaginaire est dans le réel, et que nous voyons le réel par lui' (*11,* p. 182). Butor, like the other *nouveaux romanciers,* refuses to be bound by traditional narrative logic or cause-and-effect theories of motivation. Unlike most *nouveaux romanciers* who claim incompetence in the face of specialised psychology, Butor does not duck the issues raised by developments in psychology and, by trying to incorporate certain post-Freudian concepts into his fiction, extends the range of the novel.

The thematic richness of Butor's work, its philosophical complexity frequently cause critics to neglect its self-reflexive dimension. Certainly, there is much less wilful playfulness and fewer red herrings than in the work of Robbe-Grillet or Jean Ricardou. His *mises en abyme* and transitions between the planes of reality and imagination are discreet but no less radical in their implications. The exploration of the relationships between perception, world and representation is of prime importance here as in the *nouveau roman* in general. Furthermore, the sobriety and calculation of Butor's approach only throws into relief the experimental virtuosity of his use of narrative point of view. As in *La Jalousie,* the narration of *La Modification* is a remarkably sustained example of technical virtuosity which has multiple implications about the writing and reading of a text.

6

Characterisation

Léon Delmont, a study in solipsism [22]

T H E centre of interest has definitely shifted in Butor from characterisation and plot to perceptual and philosophical concerns. Butor wastes no time on the physical appearance of his protagonist. Those details that he does give are all thematically integrated. The theme of ageing is a prominent one and an important factor in Léon's thinking – the novel could be described as the story of a mid-life crisis. Thus very early on we learn that Léon is forty-five and that he has just had a birthday. This does not stop him from painting a very flattering picture of himself as the still youthful, successful businessman who has the courage of his convictions, about to embark on a new life. This illusion is, however, somewhat dented by the inclusion of one other physical detail on page 140: 'votre crâne déjà un peu chauve'. The balding head is hardly a traditional attribute of the romantic hero. Apart from these details, Léon, like his reflection in the train window, is physically a blank.

This lack of physical detail, however, in no way precludes the creation of a psychologically interesting character. Indeed, the case of Léon Delmont constitutes an extremely nuanced study in solipsism. This is perhaps not surprising in a novel concerned with a radical transformation of the protag-

---

[22] I am using the term 'solipsism' not as a loose equivalent of the word 'egoism' with its negative moral overtones, but rather as a more neutral term referring to the restricted view of the person who confuses his own assumptions with truth and who generally fails to project himself into the situation of the people with whom he is dealing.

onist's view of the world: Léon is more than ready to have a new perspective on himself, and this perspective is supplied by the anonymous narrator addressing him so directly and insistently throughout the novel.

Until this journey Léon's view of people and places has been essentially self-centred. The narrator does not comment directly upon this fault but we see it again and again in his relationships with his wife, family and mistress. Léon seems to see himself very much as the dispenser of joy and security to those around him. He wants to graduate the announcement of plans to Cécile in order to make her savour every moment of the surprise (p. 57). He wallows in the memory of his first encounter with Cécile – the 'vin que vous lui faisiez goûter' (p. 67), the pleasure he had caused her by staying in the second-class compartment: 'ses yeux... avaient... une sorte de gaieté confiante qu'ils n'avaient pas la veille, changement dont vous vous sentiez responsable' (p. 109). On page 131 he assumes that it is his presence which gives her a sense of security and allows her to sleep. Elsewhere he is rather indiscreetly anxious to mention the presents he has given her – 'cette magnifique couverture à bandes de couleurs vives que vous lui aviez achetée' (p. 131), 'ce grand châle blanc que vous lui avez offert' (p. 57) and which figure in his imaginary picture of her. This indelicacy is further accentuated by the fact that he pays very scant attention to those objects which he has not given her and which may, for her, have a much greater sentimental value: 'une nappe damassée aux initiales... de ses parents ou même de ses grands-parents comme elle vous l'avait expliqué à l'occasion d'un autre petit déjeuner... (vous avez oublié les détails)' (p. 132). He gives little heed to what Cécile says but assumes elsewhere that she is hanging on his every word: 'Elle vous écoutait, vous regardait, vous admirait' (p. 68) and that she would want to know the details of his domestic life: 'Je croyais que tu avais envie de la connaître, de voir ma maison, mes enfants' (p. 176).

Given this preoccupation with himself, it is not surprising to find that Léon is also given to self-congratulation and self-dramatisation. His self-satisfaction as he sets out is clear:

...vous avez réussi, vous... vous avez à peu près assez d'argent, et... vous avez conservé suffisamment de jeunesse d'esprit pour pouvoir maintenant l'utiliser aux fins d'une merveilleuse aventure... Vous vous sentez maintenant au plus haut point éveillé, et vainqueur. (p. 52)

By page 80 he has convinced himself that leaving Henriette for Cécile will be an example of courage for his children, while on page 135 he presents the next few months which he will have to spend with Henriette in terms of military imagery. Of course, his resolution is not nearly as solid as he thinks, and in retrospect it is clear that he is desperately trying to keep his conscience at bay by a display of bravado. Indeed, a large part of the interest of *La Modification* comes from Butor's study of the 'doublethink' involved in infidelity, the deception clothed in the language of sincerity: 'l'on ne peut pas dire vraiment que vous la trompiez sur ce point, de telle sorte que vos mensonges à son égard ne sont pas complètement des mensonges... puisqu'ils sont malgré tout... une étape nécessaire vers la clarification de vos rapports, vers la sincérité' (pp. 40-41).

Léon is not intentionally self-centred, but he is thoughtless and insensitive in his treatment of others and has a very simplistic, two-dimensional view of the people who are closest to him. This is particularly evident at the start of the journey when Léon is so sure of his decision – he has a very clear-cut concept of the future which does not even attempt to take the views of the women concerned into account (p. 36). Again and again he simplifies and exaggerates. His description of Henriette is blatantly hyperbolic and unrealistic. He does not hesitate to pile excessive image upon excessive image (pp. 106-07). However, his view of Cécile is equally schematic. The reasons which he gives for needing her are highly suspect. He sees her largely in terms of a contrast with Henriette: 'c'est à cause de cela que je ne puis plus la supporter et que j'ai tellement besoin de toi parce que tu es une libération' (p. 177). The language he uses to describe Cécile shows again and again that he is not really treating her as a person but as a symbol of an alternative lifestyle: 'votre liberté qui s'appelle Cécile' (p. 52), 'cette gorgée d'air, ce surcroît de forces, cette main secourable' (p. 40). Elsewhere he lets slip the fact that his relationship with Cécile is also in part revenge for the 'avilissement' which his job involves (p. 207).

Léon's lack of real interest in how she thinks or feels expresses itself in the ease with which he forgets promises he has made to her, whether it be his offer to take her on a drive around the outskirts of Paris (p. 186) or his promise, on his previous visit to Rome, to have breakfast with her (p. 130). But perhaps the clearest indication that he really is not considering the wishes or feelings of either woman emerges on page 156 when he seems to think that it will be quite feasible to visit Henriette behind Cécile's back after he has brought the latter to Paris. His plan to bring Cécile to Paris is based entirely on his view of what would be most convenient for himself. Given this solipsism, it is not surprising that he feels threatened when Cécile and Henriette get on so well when they meet. It is significant and ironic that Henriette is able to make Cécile talk about herself in a way Léon has not done, 'lui posant toutes sortes de questions sur sa famille, son installation, son métier, réussissant à lui faire dire des choses que vous ne connaissiez pas encore' (p. 187). A couple of pages later it is Cécile's turn to present a very different picture of Henriette from that to which Léon has accustomed us:

> Elle a les idées bien plus larges que toi, et il te faut quitter tes illusions: tu n'as plus tellement d'importance pour elle... c'est elle-même qui m'invite, et ce n'est pas pour te faire plaisir, mais non, ce n'est pas parce qu'elle t'adore tellement qu'en renonçant à toi elle baise les pieds de celle qui te prend à elle, c'est en toute simplicité... elle te laisse toute liberté (p. 189)

By bringing Cécile and Henriette together – largely out of curiosity – Léon temporarily loses control over the situation and we are briefly given views of the other characters which challenge his account of things.

Léon's treatment of his children is no more considerate. He cannot easily put up with anything or anyone who does not conform to his wishes. Although his daughter is approaching adulthood, he still has not completely got over the fact that his first-born was not a son (p. 50). He has a stylised, hackneyed image of what family life should be and cannot accept any deviation from it: 'Ils sont vraiment au mauvais âge, ayant perdu la grâce et le charme des petits que l'on retrouve le soir pour s'amuser avec eux comme avec de merveilleux jouets' (p. 79). He has an equally simplistic and idealistic conception of how smoothly his relationship with Henri will develop after he has left his mother (p. 155). This is, of course, belied by the irritation which the boys caused him before he sets out on his journey: 'les chamailleries des garçons qui devraient pourtant à leur âge être devenus capables de se supporter mutuellement' (p. 25). But perhaps the greatest irony of this last remark is that it is equally applicable to Léon whose own level of tolerance is very low indeed. Furthermore, it seems unlikely that his relationships with his children will improve if he treats them as insensitively as he did on the occasion of his birthday. He did not even have the grace to take the wallet they gave him to Rome with him but left it lying on the dressing-table at home (p. 53). At the end of the day there is very little difference between his treatment of his family and of Cécile.

Léon's relationships with other people are only sketched in. However, the few glimpses which we are given only confirm the negative impression elsewhere. Right at the beginning of the book he shows an excessive irritability in the instant dislike which he takes to one of the other passengers (pp. 22-23). A few pages later reference is made to a threatening letter which he has sent to an employee whose name he does not even remember. The self-congratulation which we have already noticed is seen to depend partly on a feeling of power over the fates of others, whether they be his subordinates, his wife or his mistress. His self-esteem seems to be based on a sense of superiority. Thus although he imagines that some of the other passengers have a similar adulterous secret, he can only imagine it as being a sordid variation of his own (p. 104).

The picture presented of Léon is on the whole, then, a rather negative one. However, one of the most interesting and brave things about the book is the absence either of a straight-forward moral condemnation of him or a marked moral improvement on the character's part. Léon's change of heart does not involve a recognition of his own selfishness and obtuseness and a resolution to do better. Indeed, on page 274 he recognises that he will carry on seeing Cécile regardless of her welfare. Butor's didacticism is not to be confused with facile moralism. His main purpose in the characterisation of Léon is to consider the broad issue of the way in which we perceive the world and other people in general – the extent to which we see them as extensions of our own wishes, the ways in which we simplify them when we describe them:

> Le récit nous donne le monde, mais il nous donne fatalement un monde faux. Si nous voulons expliquer à Pierre qui est Paul, nous lui racontons son histoire: nous choisissons parmi nos souvenirs, notre savoir, un certain nombre de matériaux que nous arrangerons pour constituer une 'figure', et nous savons bien que... le portrait que nous avons fait est à certains égards inexact. (*11*, p. 110)

Our memory of those we know is selective, our opinion subjective and our perception intermittent. Léon is not 'guilty' of presenting a false picture of Cécile and Henriette; it would be impossible for any one individual to present a complete and objective image of anyone else. Léon's irritation and selfishness are unpleasant, and Butor takes a risk in attributing them to his protagonist, but ultimately they are very common human failings recognised by most readers in themselves. Butor is not inviting judgement on a particular character – the second person pronoun goes beyond Léon to offer us a perspective on the *mesquinerie* affecting the way in which all human beings treat one another. There is no easy reform possible, but the work of literature serves as a modest catalyst in our understanding of the way in which we operate.

Cécile and Henriette

The reader who tries to carry out a detailed analysis of Cécile and Henriette will encounter quite severe problems. We know very little of their lives outside their relationship with Léon. We have no idea of what Henriette does when Léon is at work, what Cécile does when he is in Paris. We know very little of their background or interests. We see of them only what Léon sees, and the view that we are given is extremely biased and coloured by a desire to justify himself on Léon's part. For a substantial part of the book, Henriette is associated with stagnation, drabness, habit and religious bigotry (pp. 16, 34-35, 81, etc.), while Cécile seems to epitomise energy, colour, renewal and open-mindedness (pp. 40, 52, 94-95, 109). This opposition is undermined in the course of the novel. Gradually more pleasant memories of the early days with Henriette surface and we see that the fervent Catholicism which marked Henriette's second trip to Rome did not figure in the honeymoon and that it is in part Léon's fault that she has turned to religion since. Similarly as the novel proceeds, it becomes clear that all is not satisfactory in the relationship with Cécile, that her pagan open-mindedness is itself based on an intolerance of Catholicism and that when removed from the context of Rome, she loses the 'specialness' she had for Léon.

That such an about-turn is possible demonstrates clearly that Léon has not really tried to know and understand the two women. They are simply representatives of a dichotomy within him. That Léon is drawn by sexual attraction rather than by Cécile as a person emerges quite clearly in his reaction to the other women in the carriage. He notes in great detail the movements of 'Agnès' (who reminds him of Cécile) every time she leaves or enters the compartment, paying particular attention to the way in which she brushes against him:

> Vous voyez la moitié de la robe d'Agnès, puis sa jambe qui se lève, décrit un arc hésitant... sa main s'appuie sur votre

épaule, puis sur le dossier à côté. Elle se retourne, pivote sur le talon qu'elle a réussi à faire entrer, le bord de sa jupe étalé sur votre pantalon, vos genoux serrés entre les siens, une grimace se peignant sur son visage... (p. 271)

Léon's reaction to the woman who falls asleep and leans against him is equally significant. The process as the woman's head falls on to his shoulder is painstakingly recorded in very sensuous terms (pp. 130, 231-32, 255, 259, 271). His desire expresses itself most forcefully on page 262 where he wants to nibble this stranger's neck and put his hand down her blouse. What is most interesting perhaps is that while he wants to become physically intimate with a complete stranger, on the trip back from Paris with Cécile, he tried to forget that he knew her (p. 259). From this it is clear that Léon is not concerned about Cécile as an individual – she is primarily a sex-object, a representative of sensuality.

Henriette is likewise simplified in his mind to become the representative of Catholicism, the obstacle to his passion for a younger woman. However, with Henriette Léon has to deal with competing images – the Henriette of the two visits to Rome. There is the religious fanatic of the second visit but there is also the Henriette of the honeymoon. What is particularly interesting is the evocation of the consummation of their marriage in terms of the pagan gods (p. 269) which in St Augustine represented the perilous attraction of the flesh. At the time of their marriage Henriette was as desirable as Cécile is now. Classical Rome is associated with sensuality and young women, whether they be his wife, his mistress or a stranger on the train: 'Pourquoi de Vénus et de Rome? Quel est le rapport entre ces deux choses?' (p. 270). But Henriette alone brings together both the sensual and Christian associations of Rome and it is for that reason rather than for any personal quality that he stays with her.

THE OTHER CHARACTERS

The secondary characters in *La Modification* – who are made up mostly of Léon's travelling companions – are given an unusual treatment in that very little is known or learned about them in the course of the novel. Traditionally, the fictional journey was a way of bringing together a motley crew of individuals, each with their different backgrounds and views which they proceeded to recount in the course of the journey. *La Modification* is a variation on this stories-within-a-story framework. However, as in Robbe-Grillet's film *Trans-Europe-Express* where a script-writer evolves a number of possibilities for his next film, taking one of his fellow travellers as a point of departure, Butor is using this archetypal structure to draw attention to the process by which a fiction is created. The often quite involved biographies of these characters are fictitious at two removes and very often simply variations on Léon's own situation and obsessions. Butor does not allow the passengers to engage in desultory conversation, partly because he wishes to suggest the fundamental human impulse to create a story from the flimsiest of material. The activity of composing a story is foregrounded at the expense of creating free-standing characters who speak for themselves and have a life independent of Léon.

The treatment of these 'extras' also illustrates the way in which an author will use fiction to work through his own concerns and problems. Léon's speculation about the other people in his compartment are really projections of his own situation – in the end, the multiple imaginary biographies he conjures up are so many autobiographies. The 'newly-weds' remind him not only of himself and Henriette on their honeymoon but provide him with a point of comparison in his fantasies about the forthcoming trip to Rome: 'il est possible que vous... cheminerez... longuement, lentement, sinueusement dans les petites rues obscures, votre main à sa taille ou sur son épaule, comme y chemineront les deux jeunes époux si c'est à Rome qu'ils s'arrêtent' (p. 94). By page 138 his outlook is much more jaundiced, and he pictures the future

of this young couple in terms of the decline and desintegra-
tion which has affected his own marriage. The 'honeymooners' have a convenient counterpart in the form of the old
couple who board the train and in whom Léon sees an image
of what he and Henriette will look like in later years (p. 193).
There is a further similarity in their apparent lack of communication, the old woman muttering what Léon – associat-
ing her with Henriette – imagines to be a prayer, while the
old man may be reciprocating Léon's 'authorial' interest in
him: 'il vous regarde, se sourit à lui-même, se raconte une
histoire comme si vous lui rappeliez quelqu'un' (p. 199).
Elsewhere Léon imagines that the other men in the compartment may be up to the same sort of thing as himself. Within a
few minutes of installing himself in his seat, he is speculating
about a new arrival ('à moins qu'il ne fût comme vous, en
évasion', p. 23). Much later, he wonders whether the man he
calls Lorenzo looks after his hands and nails so carefully in
order to please a mistress (p. 170). He thinks it unlikely that
the priest is going to see a woman, but on the basis of his
agitation considers it possible that he is beginning to doubt
whether or not he has taken the right road in life, may be
about to take a major decision which would alienate him too
from the Church.

This tendency to project his own lifestyle and crises on to
the people around him is both an example of his solipsism
and an indication of the hold that the social code has: even in
his moment of rebellion, Léon seems to feel the need to
belong to a particular category, to know that he is not alone
in his infidelity. However, the comparisons he draws between
the people and objects around him and his own case are
double-edged. Their presence and the associations they generate are in part responsible for his change of mind (p. 276).
The people around him and the associations they generate
relativise the two poles of his choice. Thus on page 91 the
description of the bride establishes a telling link between
Cécile and Henriette which undermines the clear-cut opposition set up between them on page 109: 'elle secoue ses
mèches, glissant ses doigts dans leur soleil de novembre
comme Cécile... comme faisait Henriette... quand elle était

encore jeune femme'. One of the things of which this assort-
ment of people makes Léon aware is the process of ageing –
Henriette would seem to be an older version of women like
Cécile and the bride; Madame Polliat is an older version of
Henriette; the old woman who appears on page 192 is an old
version of all of them. In short, the youthfulness with which
he associates Cécile is a relative and impermanent state, and
Léon is not the man in the prime of life he thought he was:
'Ces yeux qu'il a levés vers vous, soudain vous y lisez
l'étonnement et presque la pitié... comme si vous aviez vieilli
de plusieurs années depuis la dernière fois qu'il vous avait
considéré' (p. 170). Léon is made to realise his own place in
time: this journey and those around him make him conscious
of his age.

The children on the train also act on him, remind him of
his own children. The little boy accompanying Madame
Polliat looks like his son Thomas when he was younger
(p. 94). One of the two adolescents who board the train later
reminds him of his other son Henri (p. 155). The image of
mother and child offered by 'Madame Polliat' and the little
boy is a forcefully attractive image of family ties (p. 103)
which contrasts with the signs of irritability already visible in
that image of young love, the honeymooners (p. 198). In
short, Butor has radically reduced the 'autonomy' and intrinsic interest of the minor characters, reduced them largely to
the status of factors impinging on Léon's decision. Characters
are never the principal interest in Butor but are conceived in
terms of a general thematic scheme and the structural organi-
sation of the novel:

> Je pars d'une structure mais non d'une structure pure. Je
> dispose au départ d'un groupe de thèmes mais ne parviens à
> savoir ce que je veux dire qu'en travaillant sur les structures.
> Les personnages en sont des cas particuliers, des détails: ils
> seront ainsi parce que le livre doit être ainsi. Non, ils ne
> représentent jamais pour moi le point de départ. (*37*, p. 119)

This reduction has been determined by Butor's phenomenological interest, his desire to suggest the 'conditioned' nature

of our freedom. It would seem from *La Modification* that Butor subscribes to Merleau-Ponty's view whereby our decisions and choices are inextricably bound up with the people and objects of our *Lebenswelt*: 'Concrètement prise, la liberté est toujours une rencontre de l'extérieur et de l'intérieur... Nous sommes mêlés au monde et aux autres dans une confusion inextricable'.[23] No decision is ever made in a vacuum, no-one has absolute control over his future. Man has freedom of choice but is limited by his society, culture and historical situation, i.e. by the elements of his environment. In *La Modification,* the exploration of this theme through the pivotal character results in a gallery of 'figurants' who are projections of Léon's imagination and language.

[23] Merleau-Ponty, p. 518.

7

Style

P R E D I C T A B L Y , Butor's approach to style is meticulous and highly self-conscious. Nothing in Butor is left to chance and he will revise and rewrite tirelessly in an attempt to achieve the effect desired:

> Je connais des écrivains estimables qui 'tissent' ligne après ligne sans jamais revenir en arrière. Je relis; deux ou trois mots me sautent à la figure comme faux. Il faut absolument les corriger; ils sont comme des fautes d'orthographe... Ce que j'écris à la page 200 peut m'obliger à reprendre de fond en comble les dix premières pages. Il y a certainement des passages de mes livres que j'ai refaits cinquante fois. (*11*, p. 181)

For Butor, the feature which distinguishes poetic discourse from everyday functional discourse is the stylisation of the former – stylisation on every level, from the creation of an intricate global structure to the internal patterning of sentence and phrase.

Undoubtedly, one of the most important aspects of Butor's style is the attention he pays to the rhythm of his sentences. Like Simon, Butor will stretch the syntax of the sentence to its limits in order to convey the multitude of data to be taken into account in the analysis of the protagonist's situation or the proliferating connections between his story and other times and places: 'Liaisons des temps, des lieux et des personnes, nous sommes en pleine grammaire. Il faudra appeler à son secours toutes les ressources de la langue... ce qui permettra d'utiliser à plein... le magnifique éventail de formes que nous proposent nos conjugaisons' (*11*, p. 123). Thus on page 149 Léon's reluctant recognition that the relationship with Cécile has not been completely straightforward comes in an exceptionally long and complex parenthesis, the brackets translating typographically the way in which he had hitherto blocked these memories out, put them 'entre parenthèses'. Similarly, the syntactical complexity of the paragraph which opens chapter VII reflects the way in which he is trying to ward off his doubts, his attempt to reassure himself. In an attempt to explain away the gulf between himself and Henriette, Léon also ties himself up in syntactical convolutions (pp. 145-46), piling up the problems associated with his job in an attempt to rationalise his behaviour. On a number of occasions the sentences break out of the paragraph unit and span several at once. There is a good example of this on page 195 where Léon is trying to rationalise his anxiety, listing a number of possible innocuous reasons for it. The run-on punctuation expresses a fear of stopping and thinking too long about his doubts.

Elsewhere it is Butor's phenomenological interest which affects his sentence structure and punctuation and he will use them in such a way as to convey impressionistically Léon's perceptions or memories. The visual impression of the telegraph poles passing outside the window is conveyed by an unusual word order and a list of verbs separated by commas:

> Balayant vivement de leur raie noire toute l'étendue de la vitre, se succèdent sans interruption les poteaux de ciment ou de fer; montent, s'écartent, redescendent, reviennent, s'entrecroisent, se multiplient, se réunissent, rythmés par leurs isolateurs, les fils téléphoniques... (p. 14)

On pages 256-57 the broken impression of Léon's memories is conveyed by a long sentence covering several very short paragraphs. Here, like Claude Simon, Butor opts for the present participle at the expense of finite verbs in order to convey the continuing immediacy of these memories.

Elsewhere it may be an accumulation of short sentences which translates the character's state of mind. Thus on pages 165-66 the string of sentences by which Léon answers Henriette's simple question – 'Ton train a eu du retard?' – is a clear indication of his sense of guilt and a desire to exonerate himself before he is accused. This is particularly striking given the fact that he normally replies to Henriette in monosyllables only. Later, as his resolution begins to crumble, his panic is also suggested by the use of short staccato statements:

> Vous vous dites: ...je ne sais plus ce que je vais lui dire; si elle vient à Paris, je la perds; si elle vient à Paris tout sera perdu pour elle et pour moi; si je la fais entrer chez Durieu, je l'apercevrai tous les jours de la fenêtre de mon bureau, je serai forcé de l'abandonner avec une situation bien moins bonne que celle qu'elle a à Rome... Il ne faut pas y penser. (pp. 190-91)

As his panic rises, the punctuation between the statements is progressively weakened from colon to semi-colon and then to comma.

At other points it is Léon's solipsism which is revealed indirectly in the punctuation and rhythm of the paragraphs. Cécile's life-story is compressed into a couple of sentences in which the individual stages and traumas of her life are simply conveyed in a series of brief subordinate clauses. Léon's lack of real interest in her as an individual with a past is evident. The period when he and Cécile were getting to know one another is likewise accelerated (pp. 119-20). This period – normally one of excitement and discovery – is summed up in three brief paragraphs each consisting of a single complex or asyndetic sentence. These paragraphs simply lead up to the more detailed evocation of the day Léon was finally granted access to Cécile's bed. The discrepancy in narrative speeds alerts us to the primarily sexual nature of Léon's interest in Cécile.

The internal phrasing of the sentence also testifies to a high level of stylisation. Language in the *nouveau roman* is not a transparent vehicle for the objective representation of the world. It is a material whose potential patterns and recombinations have an intrinsic interest for the author. For Butor, as for Mallarmé, whom he quotes in 'Intervention à Royaumont', 'chaque fois qu'il y a effort sur le style, il y a

versification' (*11,* p. 15), and in his own work his stylistic
rigour and the concern for phonetic and semantic pattern
place him squarely in the category of what Tadié calls the
'roman poétique': 'Tout se passe comme si le roman poétique
en prose compensait l'absence de rime... par un renforcement
du système phonologique et syntaxique fondé sur les parallé-
lismes'. [24] The force of poetic language derives, according to
Butor, not from the use of 'poetic' vocabulary but from the
combination of ordinary everyday words in suggestive patterns:

> Le poète invente, en faisant jouer les mots à l'intérieur de
> certaines formes, en s'efforçant de les organiser selon des
> exigences sonores ou visuelles; il arrive ainsi à retrouver leur
> sens, à les dénuder, à leur rendre leur santé, leurs puissances
> vives. *(11.* p. 16)

> Ce sont les mots de tous les jours auxquels le poète va rendre
> leur sens, donner un sens nouveau, grâce aux 'contextes' dans
> lesquels il les saisit de façon si décisive. (*11,* p. 43)

In *La Modification,* Léon's attempt to justify his decision
to leave Henriette for Cécile is conveyed in many places
through the ternary patterning of phrases. These ternary
phrases all tend to have an emotional force and have a rising
or a falling rhythm according to whether he is referring to the
situation with Cécile or life with Henriette. Thus Cécile is
described as 'cette gorgée d'air, ce surcroît de forces, cette
main secourable' (p. 40). In her he hopes to find 'ce repos
dans ses yeux, dans ses pas, dans ses bras' (p. 207) which will
give him relief from Henriette's religiosity which 'ne fait que
s'accentuer, se resserrer, s'obscurcir' (p. 177). In contrast with
the harrassment of his life in Paris – 'cette semaine de pluie,
de cris, et de malentendus' (p. 40) – everything in Rome
seems to favour his new love, even details of the physical
setting – 'l'ombre délicieuse qui vous protégeait, vous approu-
vait, vous incitait' (p. 118). Repeatedly Léon uses several

[24] J.-Y. Tadié, *Le Récit poétique,* Paris: Presses Universitaires de France,
1978, p. 182.

words when he could use one, seemingly trying to shore up his decision with rhetoric.

Repetition is another form of syntactical parallelism which Butor uses to express Léon's emotional state. The repetition of the words 'gage' and 'secret' at the beginning of several paragraphs (pp. 40-41) not only alerts us to a certain superstitiousness on Léon's part which foreshadows his inability to abandon Catholicism but also anticipates his ultimate inability to bring the whole affair into the open and tell Henriette. On page 51 repetition translates his frustration at his claustrophobic routine:

> ... il s'agit simplement pour vous d'obtenir que les gens achètent une Scabelli au lieu d'une Olivetti... et cela sans raison véritable naturellement, jeu assez amusant parfois, jeu harrassant, jeu qui ne vous laisse pas de répit... jeu qui pourrait vous anéantir entièrement...

By page 160 this dissatisfaction with his present situation is qualified by worry about the pretence he is going to have to maintain for the next few months with Henriette. He dreads the moment when he will see her and this mounting dread is evoked once again by the repetition of 'Mardi prochain' at the beginning of successive paragraphs.

On a much broader level, the repetition or reprise of motifs is a prominent feature of *La Modification*. The circularity of the novel – Léon is going to go on to write the novel we have been reading – is reinforced by the reprise at the end of the book of a comparison from the beginning:

> ... la raffinerie de pétrole avec sa flamme et les ampoules qui décorent comme un arbre de Noël ses hautes tours d'aluminium... (p. 32)

> De l'autre côté du corridor passe la grande raffinerie de pétrole avec sa flamme et ses ampoules qui décorent, comme des arbres de Noël, ses hautes tours d'aluminium. (p. 275)

The choice of the comparison is itself thematically relevant, the Christmas tree being another example of the way in which the Christian world has annexed pagan symbols. Another motif with obvious Christian connotations is that of the serpent traditionally associated with temptation and carnal sin. Léon's repeated comparison based on it could be interpreted in terms of a deep-seated Christian guilt about sexuality, especially when it is applied to the physical attractions of Cécile: 'glissant ses doigts dans leur soleil de novembre comme Cécile dans ses serpents aux écailles de jaïs quand elle refait ses tresses' (p. 91).

The mirror or reflection motif occurs here as in Butor's other novels. On a number of occasions people and things are described indirectly in terms of their reflections, the reflection offering a distanced and defamiliarising view of things and effecting physically impossible superimpositions and combinations of objects and scenes:

> Seules les lumières des maisons dans la campagne, des automobiles et des gares, percent maintenant les reflets dans les vitres, pointant d'accents fugitifs l'image renversée de ce compartiment... (pp. 179-80)

> La lune a quitté la fenêtre, mais vous apercevez son reflet très affaibli dans le miroir entre la tête de Pierre et celle du nouvel arrivé dont vous ne distinguez pas les traits, son reflet déjà renvoyé par la vitre qui recouvre la photographie de murs crénelés et de tours. (p. 262)

Frequently Butor seems to be using the description to illustrate the complexity of perception. The mirror or reflecting surface may allow the perceiver to see something outside his own visual field but it may equally inhibit or confuse the view:

> Relevant la tête, tordant le cou... vous rouvrez les yeux et vous les fixez... sur le rectangle de verre sous lequel vous savez qu'il existe une photographie de montagnes, absolument invisible maintenant à cause des reflets jaunes du corridor; à côté, dans le miroir, apparaît par secousses, de l'autre côté de la fenêtre sur laquelle on a négligé de baisser le rideau, la lune pleine. (p. 248)

The mirror motif is also related to the theme of self-knowledge and self-recognition. Léon and Cécile's disastrous trip to Paris had undermined many of Léon's certainties and assumptions; so it is significant that his reflection in the train window appears faceless to him: 'dans les tunnels le reflet de votre visage faisait comme un trou d'ombre transparente au travers duquel vous aperceviez la fuite furieuse du roc' (p. 222). This trip, where Cécile and Henriette got on so well and Léon and Cécile so badly, challenged his self-esteem and sense of identity, and this point is made most economically by the description of the faceless reflection. Even more negative is the descripcion of his reflection in the train-mirror as he shaves towards the end of the same journey. The jaded individual he sees there is surely clear evidence that his relationship with Cécile is not the 'bain de jouvence' that he thinks and that, like Henriette, Cécile will be unable to stop him from ageing.

The novel is also punctuated by references to light – both as a physical force and as a metaphor for insight and understanding. Léon notes scrupulously the changes in the lighting around him, illustrating the way in which the physical limits of the journey have made him open to the world. However, these are of course not the only changes which take place in the book – he also accedes to a greater understanding of his situation; indeed changes in the immediate lighting conditions would seem to be partly responsible for the new relativistic perspective which he has on himself at the end of the novel. It is surely an important development when such a solipsistic individual as Léon begins to attribute to the objects around him a life of their own: 'ce bleu... restitue les objets à leur incertitude originelle, non point vus crûment mais reconstitués à partir d'indices, de telle sorte qu'ils vous regardent autant que vous les regardez' (p. 240). But it is undoubtedly in Léon's memories that light in a variety of forms – sun, moon, reflections – figures most prominently. Discreetly, throughout the text, the opposition between Henriette and Cécile is qualified by the fact that in his memory they are both associated with moonlight (pp. 68, 196, 231). One particular memory of his visit to Rome with Henriette stands out in his mind. His vivid recollection of the impression

made on him by Michelangelo's *Moses* anticipates his realisation of the importance of Christian mythology in his life:
'au milieu d'une obscurité presque totale, éclairé, seul, vio-
lemment, de telle sorte que ses cornes semblaient véritablement des cornes de lumière' (p. 171). By the end of the
journey, memory, sensory impressions and dreams have at
least partially diffused the confusion which was blurring his
vision at the outset ('vos yeux... mal ouverts, comme voilés
de fumée' p. 7). It is therefore fitting that he should express
this clarity or 'enlightenment' in terms which echo his physical journey: 'vous voyez cette lumière enfin apparaître dans
votre esprit comme la sortie d'un tunnel' (p. 247).

Another motif which is inextricably associated with Léon's
memories and the theme of perception is that of the 'tapis de
fer'. Rossum-Guyon (*37*, p. 100) has pointed out the way in
which the accumulation of debris on it serves as an indicator
of the passing of time during the journey: 'ces répétitions avec
variations ont aussi pour fonction d'exprimer la durée, le
temps vécu: le présent qui se transforme en passé'. She also
demonstrates the way in which it acts as a kind of catalyst
for memories of other trips and periods of his life (*37*, p. 202).
I would also suggest that the emphatic return to this grille is
related to Butor's phenomenological interests and his view
that we see the world through a perceptual grid composed of
a multitude of conditioning factors but in particular the
representational codes which surround us and personal codes
based on associations and memories of our own experiences.
Léon's evocation and memory of his past are not objective –
they are filtred through a grid or grille of personal associations, and appropriately Butor gives such prominence to
something which is both a banal object and an image com-
monly used by phenomenologists to explain a fundamental
feature of their theory of perception.

Finally, Butor's style is also marked by a strong graphic
tendency; he is constantly conjuring up quite startlingly
immediate visual images. This is, of course, not surprising
given the importance of the visual arts in this novel. However, the more important determining factor is undoubtedly
his phenomenological interest, in particular his desire to

make us see the banal anew. Thus he will take the most banal scene – for example, a sunny continental square (pp. 117-18) – and by focusing on the play of light and shadow rather than on individual objects will foreground aspects of it of which we were only peripherally aware but which are actually responsible for the essential impression: 'Tout deux vous regardiez le spectacle de ce peuple traversant le seuil du soleil sans interrompre gestes ni discours, allumant ou éteignant les couleurs de ses vêtements, faisant soudain jaillir des cheveux et des robes noirs plis et reflets inattendus'. In a more negative context, Léon's alienation from his domestic scene is conveyed in part by an absorption in the details of his surroundings rather than in the life and activities of the family. In a description such as the following, the details of the furniture are given as much attention as his wife:

> ... frileuse, resserrant avec sa main droite son col orné d'une piètre dentelle inutile sur sa poitrine affaissée, elle est allée ouvrir la porte de l'armoire à glace Louis-Philippe, faisant virer d'un seul coup la réflexion du plafond et de ses moulures... (sous cet éclairage diffus mais parcimonieux, comme tamisé par une quantité de lamelles d'ardoise indéfiniment délitées, l'acajou lui-même apparaissait presque sans couleur; seul un reflet de cuivre plus roux que rouge à l'angle de la moulure tremblotait)... (p. 16)

Léon sees in his family life only grey routine, and he blocks it out in favour of minute changes in the detail of his life, the play of light, scarcely perceptible modifications in his surroundings.

Butor's desire to make us look at the world with new eyes can also be seen in his use of imagery. Butor, an admirer of Baudelaire, shows the beauty to be seen in the ordinary and superficially ugly. Again and again man-made objects are described in terms of striking natural images. The losenge pattern of the 'tapis de fer' looks like the scales of some great serpent (p. 179), while the open zip of a brief-case is compared to the tiny teeth of a water-snake (p. 10). At the outset of his journey Léon is feeling very positive about the future and this expresses itself in the freshness and colour of his imagery – the shape of a piece of thread on a fellow-passenger's sock is described as a 'désordre de nuages cardés par le vent du matin' (p. 26), the railway teacups as 'bleu pâle comme un ciel de printemps incertain sur une ville du Nord' (p. 21). By half-way through his journey, the details of his surroundings – though still poeticised through imagery – are seen as much more threatening. The dirty marks on the floor are 'semblables à des nuages très menaçants de neige' (p. 141).

Butor also draws on unexpected comparisons and images to convey quite specific body sensations or combinations of emotions and sensations. Thus at the beginning of the novel he tries to circumscribe the unlabelable feeling of post-waking malaise through a simple but striking comparison: 'tout votre corps... est comme baigné, dans son réveil impar-fait, d'une eau agitée et gazeuse pleine d'animalcules en suspension' (p. 8). Much later he conveys through another simple image the sudden and sense-blunting fatigue which hits him after a long, tense day: 'toute cette fatigue accumulée tout au long des heures et des kilomètres... voici maintenant qu'elle vous menace comme un énorme tas de foin' (p. 216). This weariness is, of course, not simply physical but is also a symptom of his general emotional malaise and confusion. Thirty pages later, having decided not to tell Cécile of this visit to Rome and anticipating the feeling of oppression and inhibition he will feel, he resorts to a very unpleasant phys-ical image: 'gardant ce secret en vous comme un caillot sur votre langue' (p. 247).

In Butor the sensory and emotional aspects cannot be divorced from one another. This also accounts for the num-ber of images of wounding and scars used to describe the disharmony between Léon and both Henriette and Cécile: 'continuant à l'aimer certes, mais avec une terrible déchirure entre vous qui s'élargira douloureusement chaque fois sans pouvoir se cicatriser à cause de ce voyage même' (p. 247). Emotional decisions are not taken in a vacuum but, as we saw earlier, are inextricably bound up with immediate surroundings and sensations, the physical aspects determining emotional state and vice versa.

This disharmony between Léon and his wife and mistress is also, of course, described throughout the text as a 'fossé', 'rupture', 'fissure', 'lézarde'. This motif occurs at both the beginning and end of the book. One of the first things Léon sees when he opens his eyes in the morning is an ever-increasing crack in the ceiling (p. 16) – an image, really, of his domestic scene. In the course of the novel he is made to realise that this fissure not only marks his relationship with Cécile but is part of his own consciousness. At the end of the novel, it is revealed to be part of a general historical fissure – the gulf where a centre of values, whether they be pagan or Christian, once stood. It is this final realisation which answers the question which Léon posed himself very early on in the text about his feeling of lassitude, a feeling which he also conveyed through the image of the fissure:

> Est-ce la fatigue accumulée depuis des mois et des années, contenue par une tension qui ne se relâchait point, qui maintenant se venge, vous envahit, profitant de cette vacance que vous vous êtes accordée, comme profite la grande marée de la moindre fissure dans la digue... (p. 23)

The novel has in a sense come full circle but the understanding gained in the course of the journey illuminates at least partially the problems posed at the outset. And in the course of the novel an apparently banal detail of a modest domestic setting has been transformed into a highly complex and structurally crucial metaphor.

Language in Butor is, then, not simply a vehicle for the objective reproduction of the world. It is a material which has been highly worked by the author to create a literary artefact, a form of discourse which in its patterns and rhythms is quite distinct from the language of everyday communication. If Butor's storyline is banal (i.e. the eternal triangle) his style is on the contrary elevated and rhetorical. This 'discrepancy' has been determined by two main considerations. Firstly, the stylised representation of the ordinary, everyday experience is an effective means of defamiliarisation, of making the reader see the familiar in a new light. Secondly, the prominence of rhetorical devices in Butor's novel ensures that we are not totally absorbed in the fictional world and reminds us constantly that we are reading a *text* where reality has been processed.

8

Conclusion

LA Modification has enjoyed a wider audience than most *nouveaux romans* largely because of its blend of traditional fictional interests and a postmodernist self-reflexive dimension. It retains a very basic plot insofar as a decision is made and unmade and a change takes place in the course of the narrative. It also retains quite a strong interest in the character of the protagonist, his inconsistencies, blind-spots and moral shortcomings. On the other hand, *La Modification* is an acutely self-conscious and self-reflexive piece of discourse which deviates radically from tradition in its use of point of view and incorporates its own commentary on itself in the form of *mises en abyme*.

Unlike for example Robbe-Grillet, Butor is no iconoclast. Of all the *nouveaux romanciers* he spends the least time and effort attacking the fiction of previous ages. On the contrary there are enough points of contact between his critical essays and his own work to suggest that he sees it as part of a long literary tradition. This is completely in keeping with his subscription to the phenomenological view that human perception takes place within the context of an intersubjective cultural code.

One of the features which dominate contemporary man's cultural code is, of course, the fact that he lives in a post-Joycean era. Hence, the readiness with which the *nouveaux romanciers,* among many, cite Joyce as an influence and precursor. Of the *nouveaux romanciers,* Butor, by his range of allusion, by the complexity of his structures and by his investment of the banal with a poetic and mythical grandeur, is perhaps the most legitimate descendant of Joyce. Obviously, the scope of Butor's work is much more restricted than that of the Irish master. Nevertheless, there are important similarities. Again and again, Butor's own very sensitive comments on Joyce are reminiscent of the major preoccupations of his own work. In both Butor and Joyce the protagonists confront a world in which there is no absolute truth, where all the old philosophical systems are exposed as relative: 'les univers intellectuels de Bloom et de Stephen ont perdu l'appui d'une certitude ou d'une transcendance, ils sont hantés par les débris des systèmes anciens' (*8*, p. 256). The subversion of old assumptions and old systems is, however, in both cases clearly outweighed by the revelation of the enormous cultural wealth of our everyday life-world. In both Butor and Joyce, the banal incidents of a single day are but contemporary manifestations of timeless myths and archetypal relationships: 'Dans une journée de Dublin, il est possible de retrouver *L'Odyssée* tout entière. Au milieu de l'étrangeté contemporainent se réincarnent les anciens mythes et les rapports qu'ils expriment restent universels et éternels'.

La Modification is underpinned by a tension between the ostensible story and the rich allusiveness of the text. Like *Ulysses, A la recherche* or *Madame Bovary,* it is a book where 'la poésie de son sujet est inversement proportionnelle à celle de ses moyens'.[25] Touch one thematic chord in *La Modification* and you set off a host of reverberations in the text and the cultural codes amidst which, though we may not have been aware of it, we all live. Butor is, then, at once very modest and very ambitious in his aims. He is modest insofar as he does not try to provide an exhaustive documentary representation of contemporary society as in the case of Balzac. Nor does he pretend to any Zolaesque scientificity. However, the relationship which Butor sets up between the text and the reader is infinitely more ambitious and dynamic. Where the Realist and Naturalist sought to provide 'truths', Butor raises questions about fundamental and universal aspects of human experience. Never before perhaps has a writer's approach been more directly challenging. Button-

[25] Tadié, p. 195.

holing the reader with the opening 'vous', he does not quite let go of him at the end. The post-Butor reader will have enough food for thought to be able to say along with the author: 'J'ai du pain sur la planche pour cent ans' (*11*, p. 184).

Select Bibliography

I. Works by Michel Butor

1. *Passage de Milan,* Paris: Editions de Minuit, 1954.
2. *L'Emploi du temps,* Paris: Editions de Minuit, 1956.
3. *La Modification,* Paris: Editions de Minuit, 1957.
4. *Degrés,* Paris: Gallimard, 1960.
5. *Répertoire,* Paris: Editions de Minuit, 1960.
6. *Histoire extraordinaire, essai sur un rêve de Baudelaire,* Paris: Gallimard, 1962.
7. *Répertoire II,* Paris: Editions de Minuit, 1964.
8. *Essais sur les modernes,* Paris: Editions de Minuit, 1964.
9. *Essais sur les essais,* Paris: Gallimard, 1968.
10. *Répertoire III,* Paris: Editions de Minuit, 1968.
11. *Essais sur le roman,* Paris: Editions de Minuit, 1969.
12. *Répertoire IV,* Paris: Editions de Minuit, 1974.

II. Critical Works

13. Albérès, R.-M., *Michel Butor,* Paris: Editions Universitaires, 1964.
14. Aubral, F., *Michel Butor,* Paris: Seghers, 1973.
14a. Baril, G., ed., *Butor Studies (Kentucky Romance Quarterly,* 32.I), 1985.
15. Book-Senninger, Claude and Jack Kolbert, eds, *L'Art de Michel Butor,* New York: OUP, 1970.
16. Charbonnier, G., *Entretiens avec Michel Butor,* Paris: Gallimard, 1967.
17. Charney, H., 'Quinze, Place du Panthéon: la mythologie du vérifiable chez Michel Butor', *Symposium,* 19, 1965, 123-31.
18. Dällenbach, L., *Le Livre et ses miroirs dans l'œuvre de Michel Butor,* Paris: Minard, 1972.
19. Davies, J. C., 'Psychological realism in Butor's *La Modification*', *Symposium,* 35, 1981, 215-34.
20. Deguise, P., 'Michel Butor et le "nouveau roman"', *French Review,* 35, 1961, 153-62.
21. Greidanus, T., 'L'Imagination poétique de Michel Butor dans *L'Emploi du temps*', *Neophilologus,* 50, 1966, 307-15, 422-33.
22. Grieve, J., 'Rencontre ou piège: a footnote to *La Modification*', *Australian Journal of French Studies,* VIII, 1971, 314-18.

23. Helbo, A., *Michel Butor: vers une littérature du signe,* Brussels: Editions Complexe, 1975.
24. Jaegar, P. J., 'Three authors in search of an elusive reality: Butor, Sarraute, Robbe-Grillet', *Critique,* 6, 1963-64, 65-85.
25. Lalande, B., *La Modification,* Paris: Hatier, 1972.
26. Lesage, L., 'Michel Butor: techniques of the marvelous', *L'Esprit créateur,* VI, 1966.
27. Lydon, M., *Perpetuum Mobile,* Edmonton: University of Alberta Press, 1980.
28. McWilliams, D., 'The novelist as archeologist: Butor's *L'Emploi du temps', L'Esprit créateur,* 15, 1975, 367-76.
29. Mason, B., *Michel Butor: a checklist* (Research Bibliographies & Checklists, 27), London: Grant & Cutler, 1979.
30. Morrissette, B., 'Narrative "you" in contemporary literature', *Comparative Literature Studies,* 2, 1965, 1-25.
31. Oppenheim, L., *Intentionality and Subjectivity: a Phenomenological Study of 'La Modification',* Lexington, Kentucky: French Forum, 1980.
32. Pingaud, B., 'Je, vous, il', *Esprit,* 26, 1958, 91-99.
33. Pupitti, L., 'Le Démonstratif, signe de la prise de conscience dans *La Modification* de Michel Butor', *Neuphilologische Mitteilungen,* 67, 1966, 144-55.
34. Quéréel, P., *'La Modification' de Butor,* Paris: Hachette, 1973.
35. Raillard, G., *Butor,* Paris: Gallimard, 1968.
36. Ronse, H., 'Michel Butor: "Je ne suis pas un iconoclaste"', *Les Lettres françaises,* 13 avril 1967, 5-7.
37. Van Rossum-Guyon, F., *Critique du roman,* Paris: Gallimard, 1970.
38. Van Rossum-Guyon, F., ed., *Colloque de Cerisy: Butor,* Paris: Union Générale d'Editions, 1974.
39. Roudaut, J., *Michel Butor ou le livre futur,* Paris: Gallimard, 1964.
40. ———, 'Répétition et modification dans deux romans de Michel Butor', *Saggi et ricerche di letteratura francese,* 8, 1967, 309-64.
41. Roudiez, L., 'Michel Butor: du pain sur la planche', *Critique,* 20, 1964, 851-62.
42. ———, *Michel Butor,* New York: Columbia University Press, 1965.
43. ———, 'Problems of point of view in the early fiction of Michel Butor', *Kentucky Romance Quarterly,* 18, 1971, 145-49.
44. St. Aubyn, F. C., 'Entretien avec Michel Butor', *French Review,* 35, 1962, 12-22.
45. ———, 'Michel Butor and phenomenological realism', *Studi Francesi,* 6, 1962, 51-62.
46. Simon, J. K., 'A view from the train: Butor, Gide, Larbaud', *French Review,* 36, 1962, 161-66.
47. Spencer, M. C., *Michel Butor,* New York: Twayne Publishers, 1974.
48. ———, 'Myth and culture in Butor and Robbe-Grillet', *Australian Universities Modern Language Association,* 1977, 18-29.
49. Waelti-Walters, J. R., *Michel Butor,* Victoria, B. C.: Sono Nis Press, 1977.

CRITICAL GUIDES TO FRENCH TEXTS

edited by

Roger Little, Wolfgang van Emden, David Williams